4th Grade
Building Life Castles

by Cherie Noel

Positive Action Bible Curriculum

4th Grade: Building Life Castles

Copyright © 1990, 2005 by Positive Action For Christ, Inc., P.O. Box 1948, 833 Falls Road, Rocky Mount, NC 27802-1948. All rights reserved. No part may be reproduced in any manner without permission in writing from the publisher.

First Edition Published 1990
Second Edition Published 2005

Printed in the United States of America

ISBN: 1-929784-60-0

Author: Cherie Noel
Curriculum Consultant: Helen Boen
Editors: Steve Braswell and Ben Wright
Layout and Design: Shannon Brown
Artwork: Del Thompson

Table of Contents

Lesson 1	Who Is Jesus Christ?	5
Lesson 2	God's Promises Come True	11
Lesson 3	The Boy Jesus	15
Lesson 4	Victory Over Temptation	19
Lesson 5	The Land Where Christ Lived	23
Lesson 6	Miracles in Galilee and Samaria	27
Lesson 7	Christ Reveals His Power	31
Lesson 8	Responses To Christ's Power	35
Lesson 9	Christ Teaches Parables	39
Lesson 10	Christ Teaches About Salvation	43
Lesson 11	The Disciples Of Christ	47
Lesson 12	The Crucifixion Of Christ	51
Lesson 13	The Resurrection Of Christ	57
Lesson 14	Who Is The Holy Spirit?	61
Lesson 15	What The Spirit Does For Us	65
Lesson 16	The Fruit Of The Spirit	69
Lesson 17	Who Controls Your Life?	73
Lesson 18	Having Confidence In The Lord	77
Lesson 19	God's Concern For You	81
Lesson 20	Your Inner Character	85
Lesson 21	Humility: Doing Things God's Way	89
Lesson 22	Learning To Be Submissive	93
Lesson 23	Learning To Obey	97
Lesson 24	Learning To Trust God	101
Lesson 25	A Forgiving Spirit	105
Lesson 26	Making Wise Choices	109
Lesson 27	Compassion For Others	113
Lesson 28	Courage To Stand Alone	117
Lesson 29	Saul, The Persecutor	121
Lesson 30	Saul's Conversion	125
Lesson 31	Paul's Missionary Journeys	129
Lesson 32	The Earthquake At Philippi	133
Lesson 33	Paul Faces Opposition	137
Lesson 34	Paul's Final Journeys	141
Lesson 35	The Character of Paul	145
	Music Curriculum	147
	Scripture Memorization Sheet	160

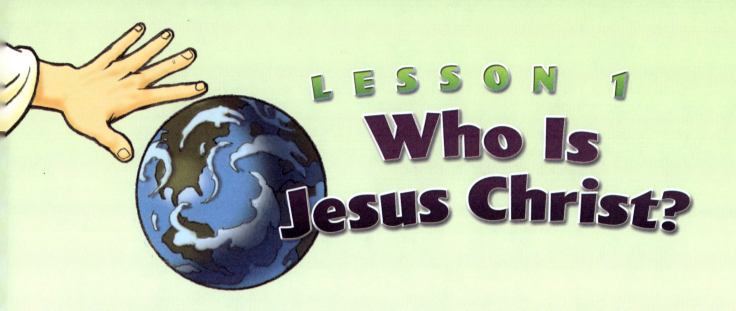

LESSON 1
Who Is Jesus Christ?

VOCABULARY

While most people think that the Lord Jesus Christ had His "beginning" when He came as a little baby to be born in the stable at Bethlehem, this is not so! It is true, as the books of Matthew and Luke tell us, that Jesus was born of the virgin Mary and that she laid him in the manger in Bethlehem, but God tells us much, much more about His Son. God says that the Lord Jesus Christ has always existed. This means that there never was a time when the Son of God did not exist.

Jesus Christ: The True God

✏ First, find 1 John 5:20. According to this verse, who is the true God? _____

✏ Now turn to John 1:1–3 and 14 and answer the following questions from these verses:

1. How long has the Word existed? _____

2. Who was the Word? _____

3. What other verse in the Bible begins with the words "in the beginning"? _____

4. According to John 1:3, who made all things? _____

Genesis 1:1 says God is the Creator. John 1:3 says that the Word made all things. Since the Word made all things, and the one who made all things is God, and Jesus is the true God, we know that Jesus created all things.

We have learned that Jesus Christ is the true God. He has always lived. We can also see the deity of Christ in the many names given to Jesus that are found in just one chapter in the Bible: John 1. The Bible is filled with hundreds of such references.

✏️ Fill in the squares below with the names of Jesus found in these verses.

John 1:1	The ☐☐☐☐
John 1:1	☐☐☐
John 1:4	The ☐☐☐☐☐ of ☐☐☐
John 1:9	The ☐☐☐☐ ☐☐☐☐☐
John 1:17	☐☐☐☐☐ ☐☐☐☐☐☐
John 1:23	The ☐☐☐☐
John 1:29	☐☐☐☐☐
John 1:29, 36	The ☐☐☐☐ of ☐☐☐
John 1:38	☐☐☐☐☐☐ (which means _____)
John 1:41	The ☐☐☐☐☐☐☐
John 1:45	☐☐☐☐☐ of ☐☐☐☐☐☐☐☐
John 1:49	The ☐☐☐☐ of ☐☐☐☐☐☐
John 1:51	The ☐☐☐ of ☐☐☐

The Old Testament is filled with names of Jesus Christ. Fill in the puzzle with names used in just one Old Testament verse: Isaiah 9:6.

Word List

Child | God | Son | Father | Wonderful | Prince | Counselor | Government

Across

3. A _____ is given to us.
4. The everlasting _____
7. He will be called Wonderful _____.
8. A _____ is born to us.

Down

1. The _____ of Peace
2. The _____ will be on His shoulders.
5. His name shall be called _____ Counselor.
6. The mighty _____

Jesus Christ: The Story Of His Birth

The beautiful story of the birth of Christ is found in Luke 2:1–20. Read the story and answer the questions below.

- Why did Mary and Joseph travel to Bethlehem when the baby was due to be born?
  _____
  _____

- Why was Jesus laid in a manger from which the animals ate? _____
  _____

- Who were the first ones to hear about the coming of Jesus? _____

- How did God tell the shepherds that their Savior had come? _____
  _____

- What did the angels tell the shepherds? _____
  _____

- Where did the shepherds find Jesus? _____

- What did the shepherds do after they had seen the Christ child? _____
  _____

Building Your Life Castle

✏️ Find 1 John 4:14. Who sent the Son into the world? _____

✏️ We have already learned that Jesus was the Creator and the one true God. The Christ child born in a stable in Bethlehem was this same God. According to this verse, why is it important for your life that the true God was born?

_____

_____

_____

LESSON 2
God's Promises Come True

VOCABULARY

✏️ In the last lesson, we learned that Jesus and the Word of God are the same. Before we begin this lesson, write the meaning of the following words. This will help you to understand the ideas that will be discussed.

- God-breathed (Inspiration): _____
  _____

- Prophecy: _____
  _____

- Testament: _____

The Bible is the complete story of Jesus Christ. God used many different men to write down His Word. He wrote the Bible by "inspiring" men, or giving His message to them and causing them to write His Word. Every word of the Bible is the Word of God.

The Bible can also be seen as a book of books. The whole Bible is made up of 66 books divided into two parts. These are the Old Testament and the New Testament. The Old Testament contains 39 books, and the New Testament contains 27. Many of the Old Testament books are very large.

The Old and New Testaments tell of the promise of God to mankind. The Old Testament is a preparation for the coming of Jesus into the world. It prophesies (or foretells) the story of Christ on earth. The New Testament begins with the birth of Christ and fulfills everything that was told (or prophesied) about Jesus in the Old Testament.

The Old Testament continually promises, "Christ will come." The New Testament says, "Christ has come. Believe in Him."

✏️ Now, in your own words, explain the difference between the Old and the New Testaments.

_____
_____
_____

Prophecies Fulfilled Concerning Christ's Life

✏️ There were hundreds of prophecies made about the life of Christ in the Old Testament. The following prophecies tell us things about Christ's life. Look up the Old Testament verse and then read the corresponding New Testament passage. Tell what prophecy was fulfilled in each pair of references.

	Old Testament	New Testament	Prophecy fulfilled
1.	Micah 5:2	Matthew 2:1	
2.	Jeremiah 31:15	Matthew 2:16–18	
3.	Hosea 11:1	Matthew 2:13–15	
4.	Isaiah 61:1	Luke 4:16–21	
5.	Zecharaiah 9:9	Matthew 21:1–10	

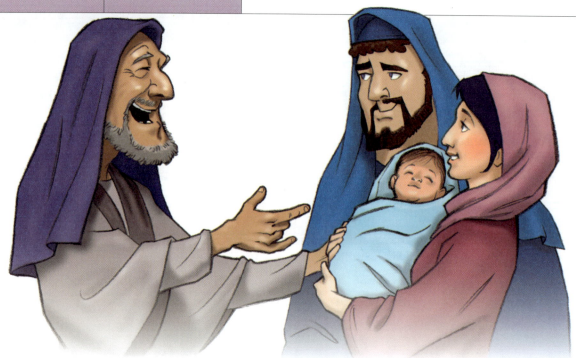

Prophecies Fulfilled Concerning Christ's Trial And Crucifixion

In a few weeks we will be studying about Jesus' death on the cross. For now, you need to learn that hundreds of prophecies were also made about His trial and crucifixion. Again, look up the prophecy made in the Old Testament verse, and see how that prophecy was fulfilled in the New Testament. Next, tell how each prophecy was fulfilled. Remember as you study that these are only five of the hundreds of prophecies that were made.

Old Testament	New Testament	Prophecy fulfilled
Zechariah 11:12–13	Matthew 26:15	
Isaiah 53:7	Matthew 27:12–14	
Psalm 22:18	Mark 15:24	
Psalm 34:20	John 19:36	
Isaiah 22:16	Luke 23:50–53	

Building Your Life Castle

✏️ Why do you think God took so much care to explain so much about His Son, Jesus, before He was born? _____

_____

_____

_____

✏️ Why is it important for us to learn about the Old Testament prophecies? _____

_____

_____

_____

✏️ Why are they important for your life? _____

_____

_____

_____

LESSON 3
The Boy Jesus

VOCABULARY

| |
| |
| |

Growing Up In Nazareth

Very little has been written about the life of Christ when He was young. This was because He was under the care and guidance of Joseph and Mary, just as you are under your parents in God's chain of command.

Jesus Christ grew up in Nazareth, which was a very small village. Boys and girls in Bible times learned to be obedient to their parents and learned to do many chores to help. The girls did not go to school but stayed with their mothers and learned to do all the household chores. They helped their mothers prepare the meals. The girls went to the village well to pull up water for household use.

On weekdays the boys went to the synagogue, which served as the grade school. They learned to read and write and do arithmetic. A boy learned to read from Old Testament scrolls. For writing he used a sharp stick on wax tablets or wrote with his finger in the sand. The boys sat on the floor near the teacher. Like all Jewish boys, before He was four years old, Jesus had been taught to honor and obey God. Long before boys went to school, they memorized prayers and verses from the Old Testament.

✏️ Read Matthew 2:19–23 to learn how Jesus spent the earliest years of His life. Then fill in the blanks below.

Jesus lived in _____ until _____ died. Then _____ and _____ took Jesus to the land of _____. When they heard that Herod's _____ was now the ruler, God told them to take Jesus to live in _____, a city in Galilee. This was a fulfillment of an Old Testament _____.

✏️ Read Luke 2:40 to see what God says about the growth of Jesus Christ when He was about your age. In the space below, explain what this verse teaches about how Jesus grew.

_____

_____

Four Areas Of Growth

✏️ Read Luke 2:52. This verse lists four areas in which Christ grew. These are also four areas in which we must grow and are listed on the chart below. Place each of the following items in the correct column:

Learning to read	Loving people	Keeping healthy	Worshiping God
Learning to write	Growing stronger	Growing taller	Thinking of others first
Pleasing God	Learning about nature	Memorizing Bible verses	Making others happy

Wisdom	Physical stature
Favor with God	**Favor with people**

✏️ Which is the one area of growth over which you have very little control? _____

✏️ List the area(s) of growth with which you are having the most problems. _____

_____

16

Obeying Those In Authority

Many times boys and girls do not show proper respect to their mothers, fathers, and teachers. Later in life they show no respect for policemen, government leaders, or others God has placed in authority. Read Luke 2:41–52. This is the story of Jesus at the temple when He was twelve years old. Remember that He was truly God in human form. This story shows by His attitude that He thought it was very important to respect and obey His parents and others in authority.

Jesus had passed His twelfth birthday and soon would be called a man. Jewish boys were considered to be adults after they turned thirteen years old. But just before Jesus turned thirteen, the Passover holidays came. Jewish men went to Jerusalem for the special feast days. Some girls and women went too, but the men were required to go.

After Joseph and Mary left for home, Jesus remained in the temple courts. During those days, teachers who served in the temple came out onto the temple porches to discuss God's law. Most Jewish students were not sent away to study the Law until they were fifteen. So it is no wonder that the temple teachers were surprised that twelve-year-old Jesus knew so much. But when Joseph and Mary became worried, returned to Jerusalem, and found Jesus at the temple, He left with them, gladly obeying all the adult leaders God had given Him.

Building Your Life Castle

Jesus Christ is our example, and He has never asked us to do anything that He did not do. During His early years, He set an example through obedience, which is the most important character quality for us to learn while we are young.

 Look up the verses below and tell the example He set and what He expects of us.

Obedience To Authority

The example of Christ:

1.	Philippians 2:8	
2.	Hebrews 5:8	

What He expects of us:

3.	Hebrews 13:17	

Studying To Be Wise

The example of Christ:

4.	Luke 2:52	

What He expects of us:

5.	2 Timothy 3:14–15	

LESSON 4
Victory Over Temptation

VOCABULARY

Have you ever had questions like these?

- What makes me want to do wrong?
- What should I do when I am tempted to do wrong?
- What should I do when I don't know what is the right choice to make?

This lesson will help you in finding answers to these questions in the Bible.

Who Is Satan?

Look up the following verses and then fill in the blanks:

	Verse	Jesus teaches us about Satan
1.	Ephesians 2:2	Satan is the prince of this world, the spirit _____.
2.	John 8:44	Christ told the men they belonged to their _____, the _____.
3.	1 Peter 5:8	Peter described Satan as a _____ that prowls around looking for someone to _____.
4.	Acts 26:18	Christ wants us to turn from _____ to _____ and from the power of Satan to _____.
5.	2 Timothy 2:26	We are to stay away from the _____ of the devil.

19

In Acts 5 you will find the story of Ananias and Sapphira. They sold something and kept back part of the price of the item. However, when they brought their offering to the apostles, they lied about the amount they gave, saying that it was all the money they had received from the sale, when actually it was only part of it. They sinned by lying to God. Read Acts 5:3–5 and answer these questions:

1. Who did Peter say had given Ananias the idea to lie to God? _____

2. What happened as a result of his lie? _____

How Christ Overcame Satan's Temptations

Jesus Christ is an example to us in every area of our lives. We are often tempted to do wrong, and so was He. Just before Christ entered His public ministry, the Holy Spirit led Him into the desert to be alone with God. There He prayed and thought about the great work He was about to begin. He was in the desert for forty days and nights with no food.

During His time in the desert, Satan came to Him three times. Each time he tried to tempt Jesus to sin against God. You will find the story in Luke 4:1–13. As you study this story, you will see how Jesus was tempted and how He was able to make the right decisions to stand against Satan.

3. Read verse 3. What did Satan first ask Jesus to do?
_____

Remember that Jesus had not eaten for forty days. Satan thought he could attack an area in which Jesus was weak. Satan will try that with you also. If you have a weakness, that is where Satan will probably tempt you. It was possible for Jesus to do this miracle, but He would never use His power to please Satan.

4. Read verse 4. Jesus answered Satan with the words from this Bible verse by saying that man does not live on _____ alone, but by every _____ of God. These words are from Deuteronomy 8:3.

5. Read verses 5–7. Next Satan promised to give Jesus worldly power and fame if He would promise to _____.

6. Read verse 8. Again Jesus answered by quoting Scripture. Deuteronomy 6:13 teaches us that we are to _____ the Lord our God and serve Him only.

20

Read verses 9–11. Once again Satan tried to get Jesus to sin. It was important to Satan for Him to sin. If Jesus had sinned even once, He could not save us from sin; and the purpose for His coming to earth would have been ruined.

Taking Jesus to a high place, Satan urged Him to jump. Down below, in the temple courtyard, Jewish worshipers were coming and going. They looked for a Messiah to come from God in some great way and lead them. If Jesus Christ now dropped from the sky into their place of worship, they would have hailed Him at once as their leader. "Jump!" Satan urged, "because God's angels can hold You up." Here Satan even used Psalm 91:11–12 to try to persuade Jesus. But Satan left out some important words, trying to get Jesus to do what he wanted.

✏️ Compare these two passages and write down the words that Satan left out.

1. _____

Jesus would not do this because this was not the kind of leader the world needed at that time. God had sent His Son to die on the cross for our sins. It was not yet time for Him to come as a King. Jesus was again firm with Satan. Read verse 12. Again He used a Bible verse to defeat Satan (Deuteronomy 6:16). This verse teaches that we are not to put the Lord our God to the test.

✏️ Remember: In each instance, what did Jesus do to rebuke and defeat Satan?

2. _____

Building Your Life Castle

✏️ We began this lesson with three questions. Here are the same three questions. See if you can answer them.

3. What makes me want to do wrong? _____

_____

4. What should I do when I am tempted to do wrong? _____

_____

5. What should I do when I don't know what is the right choice to make?

_____

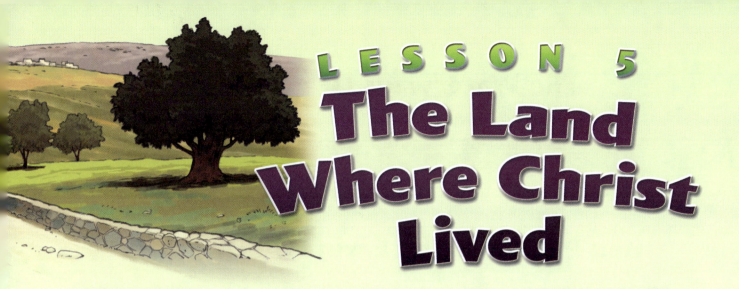

Lesson 5
The Land Where Christ Lived

VOCABULARY

It helps us to understand the life of Christ better if we understand more about the land in which He lived. Jesus lived and traveled in the land of Palestine when He was on the earth. First, with your teacher's help, find Palestine on a world map. Find Egypt on a world map also. Jesus was taken to Egypt when He was a child, as you will see during this map study.

The Regions Of Palestine

Palestine is divided into three areas. On the map, notice the names of the three regions that were familiar to Christ in His life. Turn to the map section in your Bible and see if you can find these areas there also.

- The region in the north was called Galilee. This is the area in which Christ grew up.

- The central region is named Samaria. The Jews hated the Samaritans who lived in this region. When Jews had to travel from Galilee to Judea, they often traveled around Samaria so they would not have to deal with the Samaritans. Christ, however, was not afraid to travel through Samaria. He helped a Samaritan woman to understand salvation. He also told a great parable using a Samaritan. It is called the parable of the Good Samaritan.

- The southern region is Judea. This is where the larger cities were located. This is where the capital city of Jerusalem was found. Jerusalem is where Christ was crucified and resurrected from the dead.

The Waterways Of Palestine

Next, notice on the map the key waterways that surround the land of Palestine.

- Mediterranean Sea (In Christ's time, this was called the Great Sea.)
- Dead Sea
- Jordan River
- Sea of Galilee

Key Places In The Early Life Of Christ

Now follow the early life of Christ. Write in the names of the places on the map at the end of this lesson, matching the number on the map with the number in the chart below. Then complete the rest of the chart.

	City	Verses	Explain what happened here
1	Bethlehem	Matthew 2:1	
2	Egypt	Matthew 2:13–14	
3	Nazareth	Matthew 2:19–23	
4	Jerusalem	Luke 2:42–47	
5	Jordan River	Matthew 3:13–17	
6	Wilderness of Judea	Matthew 4:1–11	

The Miracles In Judea

Below are listed several cities in the region of Judea where Christ performed miracles. Write in the names of these places on the map at the end of this lesson, matching the number on the map with the number in the chart below. Then complete the rest of the chart.

	City	Verses	Description of the miracle
4	Jerusalem	John 5:1–9	
7	Bethany	John 11:1–46	
8	Jericho	Mark 10:46–52	

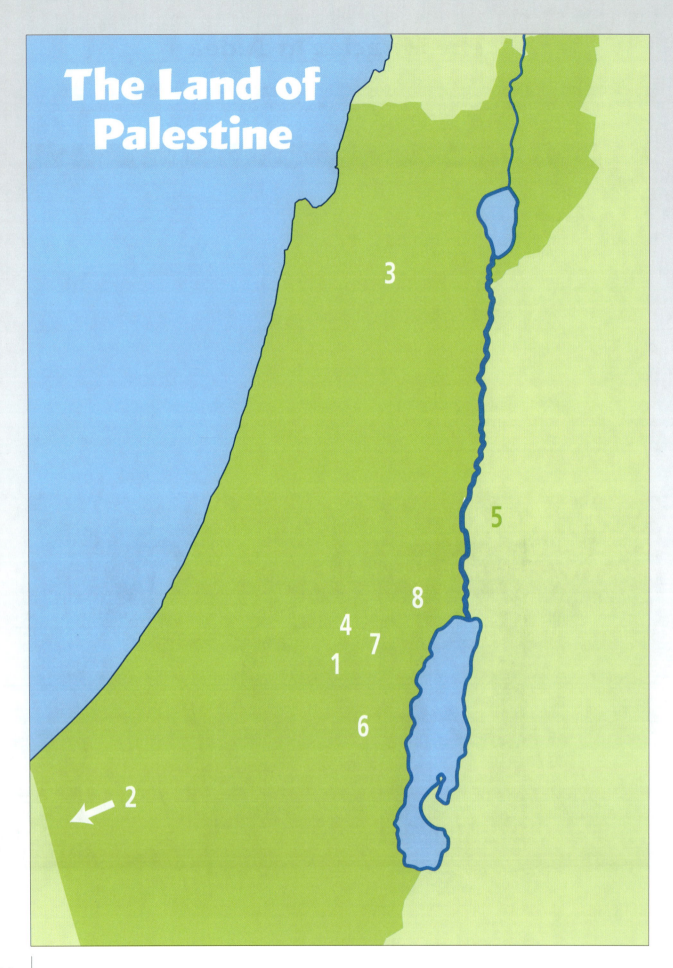

LESSON 6
Miracles In Galilee And Samaria

VOCABULARY

Jesus Christ lived in Nazareth with Joseph, Mary, His brothers, and His sisters until He was about thirty years old. Then He began His public ministry. This ministry lasted only about three years. During this time, Jesus performed many miracles. The purpose of these miracles was to show that He was truly the Son of God. When He died on the cross, many people recognized that God had been with them and was now dying for them.

As we learned in our last lesson, the country in which Christ traveled was divided into three regions. List these three regions in the following blanks:

1. The northern region: _____

2. The central region: _____

3. The southern region: _____

The Jews did not travel in Samaria. The Jews were enemies with the Samaritans and did not have anything to do with them. This is why very few miracles took place in this area. Most of the miracles took place in Galilee and Judea.

Notice the map at the end of this section. Listed on the next page are places in which Christ performed miracles in the regions of Galilee and Samaria. Write in the names of these places on the map, matching the number on the map with the number in the chart on the next page. Then complete the rest of the chart.

27

	City/Place	Verses	Description of the miracle
1	Cana	1. John 2:1–11	
		2. John 4:46–54	
2	Capernaum	3. Matthew 8:5–13	
		4. Matthew 17:24–27	
3	Sea of Galilee	5. Matthew 8:23–27	
		6. Matthew 14:25	
4	Bethsaida	7. Mark 8:22–26	
5	Gadara or Gergesa	8. Matthew 8:28–34	
6	Samaria	9. Luke 17:11–19	

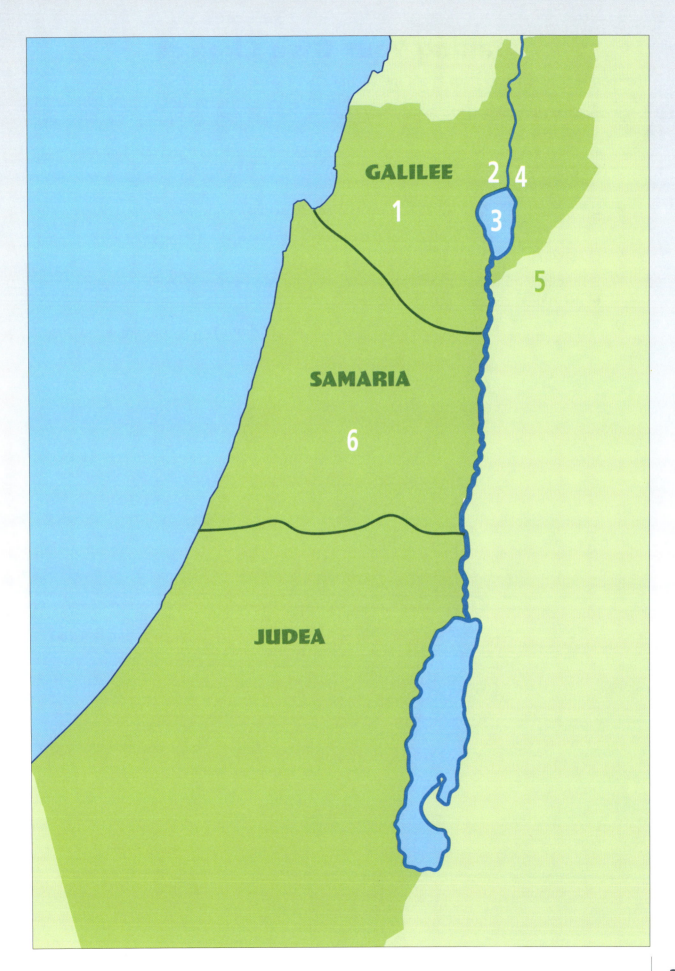

Making Your Own Choices

The more you continue to study about the life of Christ, the more you will learn that learning to be like Christ means making right choices continually. The Bible teaches us how to think and act and how to make wise choices. This puzzle will help you see how to make godly choices as Christ did.

 As you fill in the puzzle below, you will find five words that will show you five important things to consider when you are trying to discern between right and wrong.

- Deuteronomy 6:18: Do what is **(3 across)** and **(5 across)** in the sight of the Lord.

- 1 Timothy 4:12: Be an example of the believers, in speech, conduct, love, spirit, faith, and **(1 down)**.

- 2 Timothy 2:15: Work hard to present yourself approved to God. Handle the word of **(2 across)** accurately.

- Titus 2:12: We should live sensibly, righteously, and **(4 down)** in this present world.

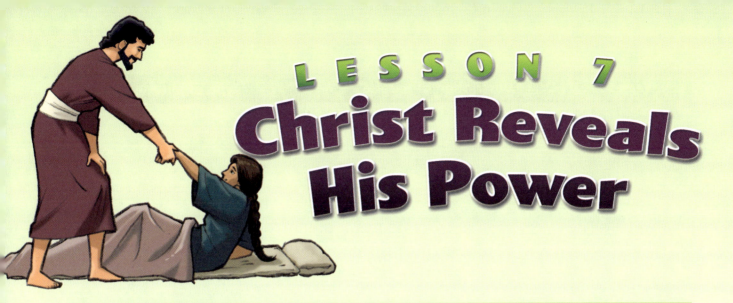

LESSON 7
Christ Reveals His Power

VOCABULARY

Christ proved that He was God in two ways:

1. By the words that He spoke
2. By the works that He did (miracles)

Christ' miracles showed the power of God because no earthly power could perform them. We are going to read in the Book of Mark about many of the miracles that Christ performed. Miracles are emphasized in Mark more than in any other Gospel.

Four Areas Of Christ's Power

Christ's miracles showed that He had control over all things by revealing His power in four specific areas:

1. Power over death—Jesus Christ raised the dead.
2. Power over Satan—Christ cast out demons or spirits.
3. Power over disease—Christ healed the sick.
4. Power over nature—Christ showed His power over the seas, the wind, food, etc.

✏️ Read the following passages out of the Book of Mark. First describe the miracle, and then tell which one of the four kinds of miracles it represents.

Verses	A Description of miracle	B Type of miracle
1. Mark 1:23–27		
2. Mark 1:29–31		

31

	Verses	A Description of miracle	B Type of miracle
1.	Mark 1:40–42		
2.	Mark 2:1–12		
3.	Mark 3:1–5		
4.	Mark 4:35–41		
5.	Mark 5:1–20		
6.	Mark 5:35–43		
7.	Mark 6:32–44		
8.	Mark 6:45–50		
9.	Mark 6:53–56		
10.	Mark 8:22–26		

The Greatest Miracle Of All

The greatest miracle of all occurred when Jesus Christ rose from the dead. This truly showed the power of God.

✏️ How does John 10:17–18 explain this great miracle of the power of God? _____

_____

Many people saw the miracles of Christ before He died on the cross. When they saw the miracles, many believed that He was God, and many did not. After Christ had risen from the dead, He appeared to many people. One disciple, Thomas, had heard that Jesus had risen; but it still seemed unbelievable to him.

✏️ Read John 20:24–31. Then match the following:

	1. Thomas was also called…	A.	…when Jesus Christ appeared to them.
	2. The disciples told Thomas…	B.	…Didymus ("the twin").
	3. The doors were shut…	C.	…that we might believe.
	4. Jesus appeared to the disciples and said,…	D.	…that they had seen the Lord.
		E.	…"Peace be unto you."
	5. Jesus invited Thomas to…	F.	…see His hands and thrust his hand into His side.
	6. The things in the Bible are written…		

33

Building Your Life Castle

Today we cannot see Christ perform His miracles. We can only read about them. We cannot call for Christ to come to us in person as He did to Thomas and convince us that He is the one who rose from the dead. But in John 20:29, Christ tells us that those who believe without seeing are blessed.

When Jesus was on the earth, His disciples saw His miracles again and again. In Mark 4:41, the disciples asked, "What kind of man is this?" How would you answer this question?

_____

_____

_____

_____

_____

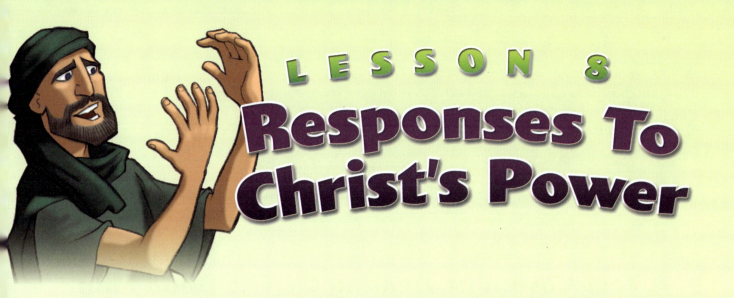

Lesson 8
Responses To Christ's Power

VOCABULARY

✏️ According to what we have studied so far, why did Christ use miracles in His ministry?

_____
_____

People Both Glad And Mad Because Of Christ's Miracles

✏️ Look up the following verses to see how different people responded to the miracles Christ performed:

1.	Matthew 12:14	
2.	Luke 4:36	
3.	Luke 5:26	
4.	Luke 6:11	

This shows that people had different attitudes toward Christ's miracles. But Christ's purpose was only to show that He was God. He used the ministry of miracles to glorify God. He would not perform miracles for any other reason.

A. With this in mind, read Luke 23:8–9. This meeting takes place when Christ was brought to trial before He was crucified. Answer the following questions about this meeting:

1. Who was glad to see Christ? _____

2. What did he hope to see? _____

3. How did Christ respond? _____

Herod wanted to be entertained. Christ always did what He did for a good reason—a godly reason. He did not perform miracles for someone's entertainment.

A Test Case: The Healing Of The Blind Man

As we have seen, every person who met Jesus and watched His ministry reacted differently. As we study about the healing of the blind man, you will see again how people reacted to Christ's miracles. Most people did not want to believe that Jesus Christ was God, and they questioned His purposes continually. Read the story in John 9:1–33.

B. Read verses 4–7 and explain in your own words what Christ had the blind man do to be healed. _____

C. There were four groups of people who were present when the man was healed. Read the verses given below and explain how each group felt about the blind man.

Verses	Group	How did they feel and respond?
1. Verse 2	Disciples	a. b. What was Christ's answer to their question?
2. Verses 8–9	Neighbors	
3. Verses 16–17	The Pharisees	
4. Verses 18–19	The Jews	

D. Who did the blind man think Christ was? See verses 30–33. _____

How Are You Responding To God's Power?

As we have seen from the ways people responded to Christ's miracles, the key to our responses to God is the condition of our hearts. God wants us to learn to have a loving heart and a loving attitude toward everyone. The Bible, however, tells us that many people's hearts are much different from what God requires. Some of the differences between godly and ungodly heart attitudes are mentioned below.

Read the verses and answer the questions.

A

#	Verse	Question	Answer
1.	Proverbs 15:13	What kind of heart makes the face cheerful?	
2.	Proverbs 28:25	What kind of person stirs up conflict?	
3.	Isaiah 35:4	What should we say to a person with a fearful heart?	
4.	Isaiah 38:3	What kind of heart can we ask the Lord to remember?	
5.	Jeremiah 5:23	What kind of hearts did the people have who Jeremiah prophesied about?	
6.	Luke 8:15	How do those who have good hearts respond when they hear the Word?	
7.	Romans 1:21	What kind of heart does a person have who refuses to glorify God?	
8.	1 Peter 1:22	With what kind of heart should we love one another?	

 God is a searcher of hearts (Romans 8:27). He knows your heart even better than you. As you look over these verses, think about your own heart attitude. Then write each of the words describing attitudes of the heart from above in the correct column below. Which group of words best describes your attitudes?

B

Godly attitudes	Wrong attitudes
1. _____ heart	1. _____ heart
2. _____ heart	2. _____ heart
3. _____ heart	3. _____ heart
4. _____ heart	4. _____ heart
5. _____ heart	

Building Your Life Castle

Christ was continually teaching lessons through His miracles. He wants us to learn something for ourselves from the story of the blind man.

✏️ Read John 8:12 and answer the questions below:

1. Who is the Light of the world? _____

2. What do those who follow Him have to keep them from walking in darkness?
   _____

✏️ In John 9:5 Christ repeated a part of that same verse. He said that He was the Light of the world. Now think through the story of the blind man once again.

3. What do you think blindness or darkness represents in the Bible?
   _____
   _____

4. Who alone can take away the darkness? _____

5. The blind man was blind from his birth—he was in darkness! In what way were you in this condition from your birth? _____
   _____

6. What did Christ mean when He called Himself the Light of the world?
   _____
   _____

7. What lesson did you learn from the story of the blind man who was healed?
   _____
   _____
   _____

LESSON 9
Christ Teaches Parables

VOCABULARY

Many times in the Gospels Jesus says words that mean, "Listen and obey"; therefore, we should take a careful look at what He is saying in His Word.

1. ✏️ What does Jesus say in Mark 4:24 that teaches this truth? _____

_____

_____

These few short words are very simple. As you hear the Word of God almost every day, be sure that you are not just a listener, but an obedient listener. Jesus Christ is the greatest teacher the world has known. He knows all things. When He speaks, we should hear and obey what He has to tell us.

2. ✏️ What does Luke 8:18 say is important about our hearing? _____

_____

- **What** you hear is a necessary part. It is the gaining of facts and knowledge.

- **How** you hear is even more necessary. This means you are applying wisdom to the facts you have learned. It means you have a right attitude about the teachings of God.

- God wants you to use the truth you hear with great wisdom in your life. Therefore, you need to pay attention to what you hear *and* how you hear it.

The Parables Teach Us Lessons

One of the ways that Christ taught us great truths and showed us how to live was through parables. He used parables to teach us the things that could help us in our lives. A parable is a story that teaches a lesson. Read the two parables in Luke 15:3–10.

1. What is lost in the first parable (vs. 3–7)?
   _____

2. What is lost in the second parable (vs. 8–10)? _____

3. What lesson is Christ teaching in both of these stories? _____
   _____

The Parable Of The Sower

We are going to study a great and important parable. Read the parable of the sower in Luke 8:5–15. As you study this parable, think and decide what has happened to the seed of God's Word in your own life.

4. What is the seed (vs. 11)? _____

5. Who takes away the seed of God's Word from people's hearts (vs. 12)? _____

Now we will study the parable part by part and see what Christ was teaching (gain facts) and how we should apply this to our lives (gain wisdom).

A Where was the seed sown?	B What happened to the seed?	C What did this mean?
6. Verse 5:	Verse 5:	Verse 12:
7. Verse 6:	Verse 6:	Verse 13:
8. Verse 7:	Verse 7:	Verse 14:
9. Verse 8:	Verse 8:	Verse 15:

Good Seed Produces Fruit

In the parable of the sower, Luke 8:14–15 talks about producing fruit. If you have trusted Christ to save you, the Holy Spirit lives within you. Verse 8 shows us that the only place that brought forth fruit was the seed sown on good soil.

✎ Now look up Galatians 5:22–23. These verses list the fruit of the Spirit. Write the parts of the fruit of the Spirit in the boxes below. This is the fruit God wants to produce in your life.

A

1.	4.	7.
2.	5.	8.
3.	6.	9.

Building Your Life Castle

Now look again at the parable of the sower, which teaches us to pay attention to how we hear.

B ✎ Which of the four examples of seed is your heart most like? _____

2 ✎ Why do you think so? _____
_____

3 ✎ How can this parable help you in your life? _____
_____
_____

4 ✎ What did you learn? _____
_____
_____
_____
_____

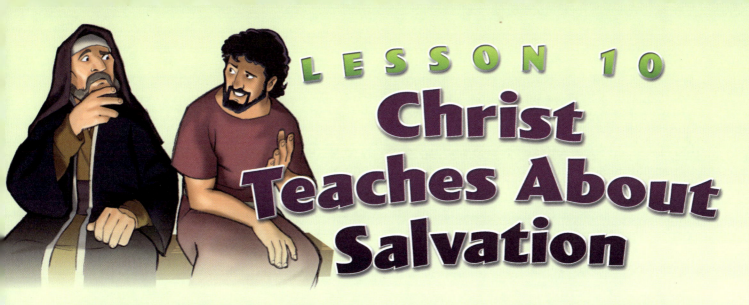

LESSON 10
Christ Teaches About Salvation

VOCABULARY

We know that Christ came to the earth to die on the cross so that we might be saved from our sins. He performed many miracles while He lived on the earth, and He taught many lessons; but His main purpose for coming to the earth was to die on the cross.

Christ's Conversation With Nicodemus

One time Christ had a talk with an important Jewish leader. This man's name was Nicodemus. Nicodemus had heard much about Christ. He had heard about His miracles and His teachings. Finally, Nicodemus had to talk to Christ for himself. Because of his high position, he came to talk to Christ at night when he would not be seen. Christ taught Nicodemus the greatest lesson of the Bible. He taught Nicodemus how he could have eternal life. Read John 3:1–8 and learn about this great lesson.

1. From reading verses 1 and 2, what can you tell about Nicodemus? _____
_____
_____
_____

In verse 3, Christ immediately told Nicodemus what his problem was. He needed to be saved. Christ told him that unless a man is born again, he cannot see the kingdom of God.

2. In verse 4, we see that Nicodemus did not understand what Christ was saying. What did Nicodemus think He was saying?
_____
_____

43

In verses 5 and 6, Christ explained that He was not talking about being "born again" physically. He was explaining that we need to be "born again" spiritually. He said that unless a man is born of water and of the Spirit, he cannot enter into the kingdom of God.

A. Now read John 3:16. Jesus also said these words to Nicodemus to try to make him understand what it means to be born again. Read this well-known verse and answer the following questions about the gospel:

1. What did God do? _____

2. Why did He do this? _____

3. What do we have to do? _____

4. What will be the result if we do this? _____

We cannot completely understand exactly how Christ gives us a new life. But we can believe it is true and that it can happen to us if we believe in Him as our Savior. Christ told Nicodemus that even he, with all his good qualities, was a sinner in God's eyes. Nicodemus had to be born again. And everyone else who wants to belong to God's family must also be born again.

B. What does the word "condemn" mean? (You may find it in your vocabulary list.) _____

_____

C. Read John 3:18. God says that if we have been born again by believing in Christ as our Lord and Savior, we are not condemned. What does this verse also say about the person who has not believed on Christ?

_____

The promise that God made to take us to heaven is unlike anything else. Once we are in His family, we are assured that we will be in heaven one day. First John 5:13 says that we can know that we have eternal life.

The Story Of The Good Samaritan

Christ also taught people how they should treat others once they are saved. In Luke 10, a lawyer asked Christ how to have eternal life. Christ replied by asking him what was written in the law.

D. The lawyer's answer was to quote from the Old Testament commands to 1._____

the Lord our God with all your 2._____, all your 3._____,

all your 4._____, and all your 5._____, and to love your

6._____ as you love yourself (vs. 27).

When the lawyer asked Christ who his neighbor was, He told the story of the Good Samaritan.

✏️ Complete the puzzle below by supplying the missing words from the story in Luke 10.

A man who was traveling from Jerusalem to Jericho fell into the hands of **(7)** _____ (vs. 30) who wounded him and left him half dead. A **(6)** _____ (vs. 31) came by; and when he saw him, he passed by on the other side. Soon a **(8)** _____ (vs. 32) came by, looked at him and **(4)** _____ (vs. 32) by on the other side.

Then a **(3)** _____ (vs. 33) came by and had compassion on him. The Samaritan went to him, bandaged his **(2)** _____ (vs. 34), brought him to an **(10)** _____ (vs. 34) and took **(5)** _____ (vs. 34) of him. The next day he gave money to the innkeeper and asked him to take care of him until he was well.

Now Christ asked the lawyer which of these was a **(9)** _____ (vs. 36) to him. The lawyer replied that it was the one who showed **(1)** _____ (vs. 37) to him. Then Christ told him to go and do the same.

Now transfer your answers to the list below, placing the answer from the blank marked "1" beside the number "1" below, and so forth.

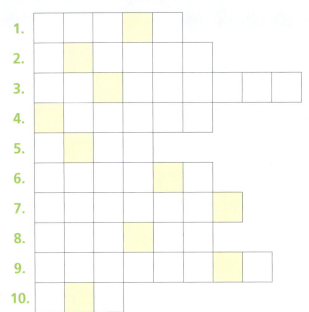

In the order in which they are highlighted, write these letters below to find the character quality Christ was teaching us to have through this parable.

Building Your Life Castle

1. Have you been born again? _____

2. Can you tell when you first trusted Christ as your Lord and Savior? _____

3. Explain what happened. _____
   _____
   _____

4. How do you know that you are trusting Him to be your Savior today? _____
   _____
   _____

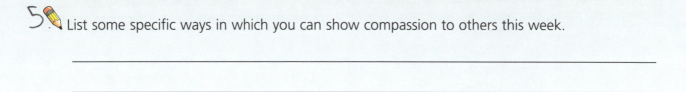

If you are not sure if you have been born again, talk to your teacher and find out how you can know that you have eternal life.

5. List some specific ways in which you can show compassion to others this week.
   _____
   _____

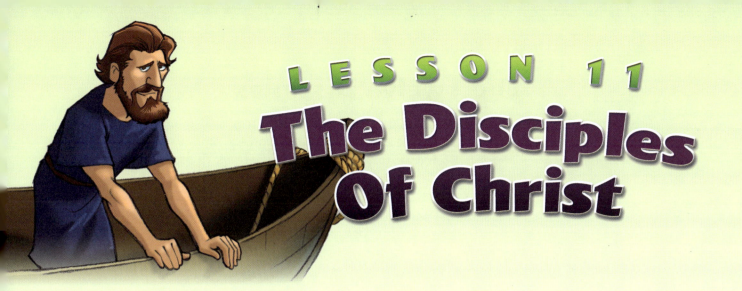

Lesson 11
The Disciples Of Christ

VOCABULARY

What Is A Disciple?

There are two meanings to the word "disciple."

- **A learner**—a student; one who receives instruction from another.
- **A follower**—one who believes in and follows the teachings of another. The men who were constantly with Christ were called "disciples." All Christians are called His disciples as they profess to learn and receive His teachings.

The original disciples of Christ (the small group of eleven men after Judas died) were also called to be apostles. An apostle was one sent by Jesus Christ to begin the church of Jesus Christ in the world.

1. Read Mark 3:14–15. Verse 14 says that He chose twelve who were to be with Him. It was important that these twelve men were with Christ because they would not otherwise have learned His teachings. How can you be with Christ to learn His teachings?

_____

_____

During the time Christ was on earth, the twelve disciples were given special power to preach, heal the sick, and cast out demons.

2. The power to accomplish these things did not come from the twelve men themselves. Where did they receive this power? _____

3. What do you think God's purpose was when He had the disciples perform these acts?

_____

_____

47

The Twelve Disciples

✏️ The twelve men that were chosen by Jesus Christ to be His first disciples were really no different from you. They were common people such as fishermen and workers. One was a tax collector. Read Matthew 10:2–4 and list the twelve original disciples that Jesus Christ called to follow Him.

A

1.	7.
2.	8.
3.	9.
4.	10.
5.	11.
6.	12.

B

Across

1. He betrayed Jesus (John 13:2).
2. His name begins with a "B" (Matthew 10:3).
4. He did not believe the other disciples when they said they had seen Christ alive (John 20:24–25).
6. His name begins with a "T" (Matthew 10:3).
9. He said he would be satisfied if he could see the Father (John 14:8).
11. He brought his brother Peter to Christ (John 1:40–41).

C

Down

1. He was preparing his nets with his brother John when he was called by Christ (Matthew 4:21).
3. He was the son of Alphaeus (Matthew 10:3).
5. He was a tax collector (Matthew 9:9).
7. He may have been a Zealot before he followed Christ. Zealots were members of a violent political party (Acts 1:13).
8. He was called the disciple "whom Jesus loved" and later wrote three New Testament epistles.
10. He denied Christ three times before the crucifixion (John 18:26–27).

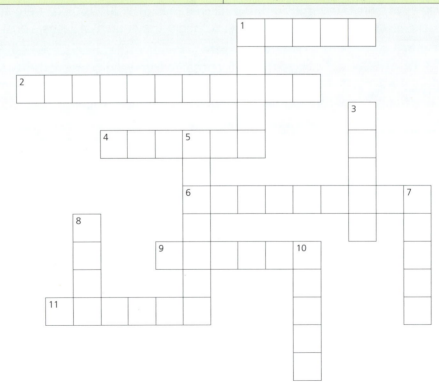

1. Now read 1 Corinthians 1:26–29. What kind of person does Christ call to become His disciples or followers? _____

Disciples Must Be Learners

The first disciples had to learn the same lessons that you and I must learn. They did not always have the faith in Christ that they should have had. Christ taught them a lesson on faith in Matthew 14:22–33. Read the story and answer the questions below.

2. What was the problem the disciples had when they were in the ship?
_____

3. Who did the disciples think Christ was when they saw Him walking on the sea?
_____

4. How did they feel? _____

5. Does this show faith or lack of faith? _____

6. What did Peter do at first that showed he had faith in Christ? _____
_____

7. Then what happened that showed his faith was not very strong?
_____

1. What did Peter cry out to Christ? _____

2. As soon as Jesus heard this cry, what was His response? _____
_____

Building Your Life Castle

3. Are you a disciple of Jesus Christ? Look at the definition at the beginning of this lesson and explain how you can tell whether or not you are truly one of His disciples.
_____
_____

4. According to what you learned in this lesson, what do you think Christ was trying to teach the twelve disciples before He sent them out in His name?
_____
_____

5. Can you give one example of how He is trying to teach you the same lesson in your life to strengthen you as a disciple?
_____
_____
_____
_____

LESSON 12
The Crucifixion Of Christ

VOCABULARY

| |
| |
| |

✏️ As we begin our study of the death of Christ on the cross, read John 10:17–18 and answer the following questions:

1. What does Christ say He is going to do? _____

2. What will He do then? _____

3. Could any man take Christ's life from Him? _____

4. Who has the power to take Christ's life? _____

5. Who has the power to come back to life? _____

6. From whom did Christ receive the command to do all of this? _____

Christ's Arrest

Our Lord came to die for the sins of the world. And although He could have prayed to His Father, and He would have sent more than twelve legions of angels (Matthew 26:53), the Lord Jesus allowed the soldiers to take Him away bound. Had Christ saved Himself from death on the cross, He could not have saved us from our sin.

✏️ Now read John 18:1–13 and answer the following questions by marking the correct answer:

1.	☐ Yes	☐ No	Judas was with the disciples.
2.	☐ Yes	☐ No	The soldiers came with weapons to take Christ.

A

1	☐ Yes	☐ No	Christ knew all things that would happen to Him.
2	☐ Yes	☐ No	Christ tried to escape from His enemies.
3	☐ Yes	☐ No	Christ's enemies were able to stand before Him.
4	☐ Yes	☐ No	The soldiers fell backward to the ground.
5	☐ Yes	☐ No	Christ wanted His disciples to be safe.
6	☐ Yes	☐ No	Christ asked Peter to fight for Him.
7	☐ Yes	☐ No	Christ's greatest desire was to do God's will.
8	☐ Yes	☐ No	Christ let Himself be bound and taken away.

Christ's Trial

Read John 18:19–40 to find out what happened at Christ's trial. Read the verses given and tell who made each statement.

B

#	John	Statement or question	Who said it?
1	18:29	What accusation do you bring against this man?	
2	18:30	If He were not a criminal, we would not have brought Him to you.	
3	18:31	Judge Him according to your law.	
4	18:33	Are you the King of the Jews?	
5	18:34	Is that what you think, or did others tell you?	
6	18:35	What have you done?	
7	18:36	If My kingdom were of this world, My servants would fight so I would not be delivered to the Jews.	
8	18:37	So are you a King?	
9	18:37	For this reason I was born, and for this cause I came into the world.	
10	18:38	I find no fault in Him at all.	
11	18:39	Shall I release to you the King of the Jews?	
12	18:40	Not this man, but Barabbas.	

Christ's Sufferings

A Look up the verses below and fill in the blanks to gain an understanding of what Christ went through when He died on the cross for us. The words will show you some of the things Christ suffered when He took our sins on Himself.

1. They _____ Him (John 19:1).

2. They _____ Him (Matthew 27:28).

3. They _____ Him (Mark 15:20).

4. They _____ on Him (Matthew 27:30).

5. They _____ Him (Luke 22:63).

6. They _____ Him (Luke 23:10).

B 1. Christ's enemies taunted Him with His true title:

"_____" (John 19:3).

2. During this torture, Christ did not open His _____ (Isaiah 53:7). When He was insulted, He did not

_____; and when He suffered, He did not

make _____ (1 Peter 2:23).

3. In spite of all His sufferings, the chief priests and officers

cried, "_____" (John 19:6).

C The following three phrases were among those spoken by Christ while He was on the cross:

1. Luke 23:34: _____
   _____

2. Luke 23:43: _____
   _____

3. Luke 23:46: _____
   _____

53

The Scene Of Christ's Final Days

Jerusalem was the religious and political capital of Israel. Here were the palaces of Herod and Pilate, who were the political leaders. Here also were the temple and the Jewish spiritual leaders. Both of these groups wanted Jesus Christ to die on the cross.

 By the numbers noted on the map of Jerusalem to the right, write in the names of the following:

1. **The Last Supper.** This is where it probably took place.

2. **The Garden of Gethsemane.** This is where Christ prayed while the disciples fell asleep. This is also where He was betrayed by Judas and arrested.

3. **The Religious Council.** They met here and sent Christ to Pilate.

4. **Pilate's Palace.** Pilate did not want to make a decision about Christ. Christ was beaten here and sent to Herod.

5. **Herod's Palace.** Herod sent Christ back for Pilate to make a decision about what to do. Pilate asked the people what they wanted. They asked for the murderer Barabbas to be freed and wanted Christ crucified.

6. **Calvary.** This place, outside of the city gates, was where the crucifixion took place.

Christ Crucified

Read the verses listed below and complete the following puzzle:

1. _____ you the King of the Jews? (John 18:33).
2. I find no _____ in Him (John 19:6).
3. A servant named _____ had his ear cut off by Peter (John 18:10).
4. Jesus Christ was made _____ through His suffering (Hebrews 5:8–9).
5. The people _____ out, "Crucify Him!" (John 19:15).
6. Jesus was a _____ (John 19:19).

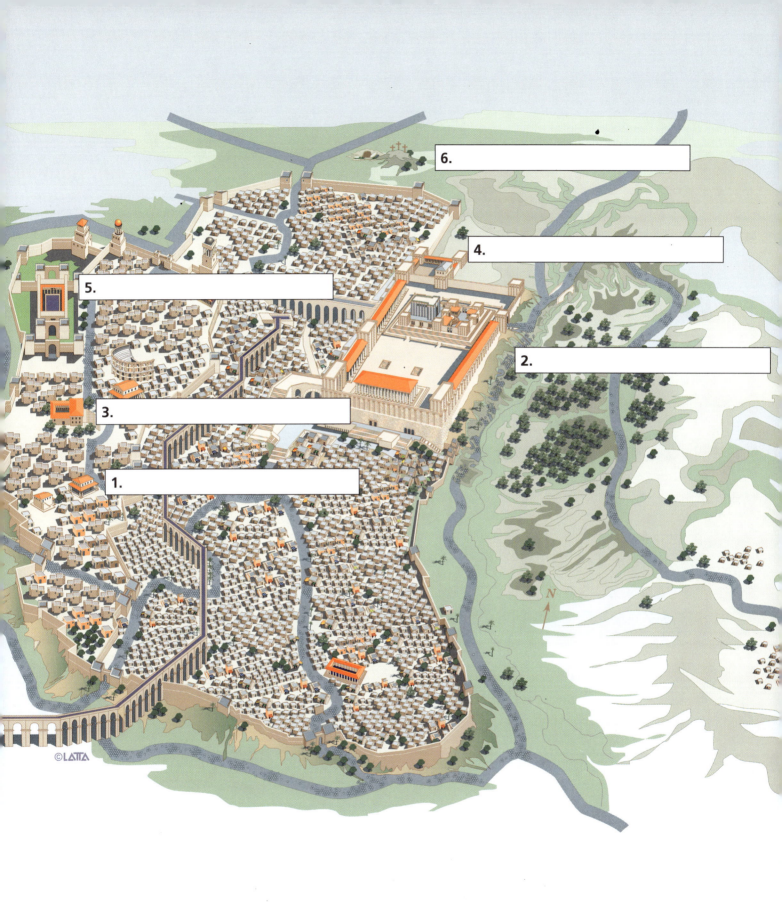

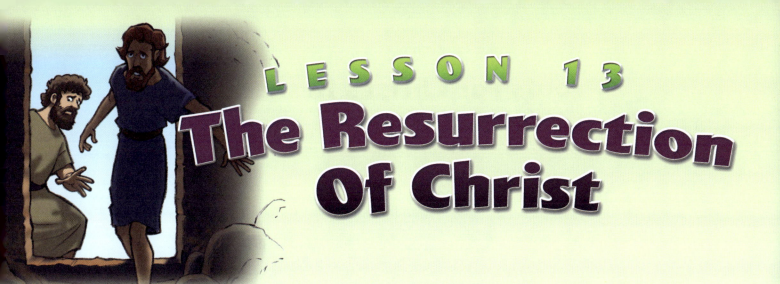

Lesson 13: The Resurrection Of Christ

VOCABULARY

_____

_____

_____

The most important teaching of the entire Bible is the fact that Jesus Christ of Nazareth died on the cross and arose three days later. Upon these facts rest all the other teachings of the Bible.

Dead, Yet Alive

✏️ Read John 20 and complete the following story by unscrambling the words beneath each blank:

When 1. _____ came early to the tomb on the first day of the week
              mrya gdaaeelnm

and found the stone taken away, she ran to 2. _____ and another
                                                    mison teerp

3. _____ and told them, "They have taken away the 4. _____,
    dilepisc   rlod

and we know not where they have laid Him!"

Later that evening 5. _____ came and spoke peace to them. Then the
                                sesuj

6. _____ were overjoyed when they saw the 7. _____.
    iiesspdcl   rold

8. _____ was not with them. He said he would not believe until he saw and
    sohtma

touched the print of the 9. _____ in Jesus' 10. _____.
                                  slain   sdnha

A week later, 11. _____ came to them again, and 12. _____
               jssue   mastho

saw Him. Now he believed, calling Jesus, "My 13. _____ and my 14. _____!"
                                                          rold   ogd

Proofs For Christ's Resurrection

A. Look again at the following verses from John 20 to find three things Mary, Peter, and John saw that made them know Jesus Christ had truly risen from the dead:

1. The _____ taken away (vs. 1)

2. The linen _____ lying there (vs. 6)

3. The cloth from His _____ folded together in a place by itself (vs. 7)

There are many who would deny that Christ is alive today. They say there is no proof. Christ was not seen by just a couple of people who may or may not have been reliable witnesses. He was seen by hundreds of people who knew about His crucifixion and death.

B. Read the verses listed below and identify the people by name or by number who actually saw Christ after His death and resurrection.

Verses	Who saw Christ after His resurrection?
1. Mark 16:9	
2. Luke 24:34	
3. Matthew 28:16–17	
4. 1 Corinthians 15:6	
5. Acts 1:1–9	

C. Read Acts 1:9–11 and explain in your own words what these witnesses saw happen.

_____

_____

_____

The Importance Of The Resurrection

If there were no resurrection and Christ had not risen from the grave, it would mean that He is still dead. We would not be able to pray to Him. We would not be able to look forward to being with Him in heaven. We would not have forgiveness for our sins. We would not be able to look forward to His return for us.

D. Read these verses and answer the these questions that explain how important these facts are.

1. 1 Corinthians 15:14. If Christ did not rise from the dead, then what would have to be said about having faith in Him? _____

2. 1 Corinthians 15:15. What kind of witnesses would the early apostles have been if Christ were still dead? _____

3. 1 Corinthians 15:17. If Christ is not raised, then in what condition do we find ourselves? _____

4. 1 Corinthians 15:18. If Christ did not rise from the dead, then what has happened to those who have died? _____

5. 1 Corinthians 15:19. What does this verse say about a Christian who does not have a risen Savior? _____

LESSON 14
Who Is The Holy Spirit?

VOCABULARY

The Home Of The Spirit

A. The Holy Spirit is a person, not a thing. You should refer to the Holy Spirit as He or Him, not it! The Holy Spirit is God. Read Romans 8:9 and you will see that this is true. In this verse the Spirit is referred to in two ways. Name the two ways below.

1. _____
2. _____

3. According to this verse, where does the Spirit live? _____

4. According to this verse, how do we know that we belong to God? _____
_____

We cannot completely understand how the Holy Spirit can be God and Christ be God and the Father be God—and yet God be only one God! But the Bible says this is so. Christ is now in heaven with God the Father and does not live within your body. But God can live inside you in the person of the Holy Spirit.

B. Now read 1 Corinthians 3:16. This verse says that when we become Christians, our bodies become the house (temple) of God. What does this verse say about who comes to dwell in the house?
_____
_____

The Holy Spirit comes to live within a person as soon as he trusts Jesus Christ as his Lord and Savior. He must first admit that he is a sinner. He must understand that he cannot go to heaven with these sins. Then he must understand that this is why Jesus Christ came to live on earth. He came to die on the cross in our place. He took on Himself our sin. If we trust Christ as our Savior and understand that He takes away our sin, we become Christians. The Bible says we are "born again." It is at this time, when we are born again, that the Holy Spirit of God comes to live within us.

61

The Names Of The Spirit

A. Just as Jesus Christ has many names that explain more about Him, so does the Holy Spirit have names that tell us more about Him. Look up the following verses and learn some of the names Scripture gives Him:

1. John 14:16 _____
2. John 14:17 _____
3. John 14:26 _____

4. According to John 14:17, where was the Holy Spirit to live? _____

5. Read John 14:26. What was the Holy Spirit to do? _____
_____

B. In your own words, explain why you think the Holy Spirit was given each of these names:

1. Comforter (or Counselor, Helper, Advocate):

2. Spirit of Truth:

C.

What the Holy Spirit did for the disciples and others	What the Holy Spirit can do for me
1. He was their Helper and gave them b _____ to speak for the Lord Jesus (Acts 4:29–31).	He will be my Helper when _____ .
2. He was their Comforter and gave the members of the early church _____ from persecution (Acts 9:31).	He will be my Comforter when _____ .
3. He was their Guide when they went out to witness throughout the **w** _____ (Mark 16:15).	He will be my Guide when _____ .

Puzzle

See if you can find how the names of the Holy Spirit fit into the puzzle. Each time the word "Spirit" is used, it has been written in for you. The shaded boxes represent spaces between words.

Comforter	Spirit of Christ	Helper
Spirit of God	Guide	Holy Spirit

LESSON 15
What The Spirit Does For Us

VOCABULARY

Not Left Alone

Before Christ died on the cross and rose again, He told the disciples that He would be leaving them. They did not understand why He would leave, and they were very sad.

✏️ Read the following verses from John 14, and you will learn what Christ said at that time.

1. John 14:1. What did Christ say to comfort the disciples? _____
_____

2. John 14:2. Why was Christ going to His Father's house? _____
_____

3. John 14:3. This promise to prepare a place was for the disciples, and it is also a promise for us. What other promise did Christ make? _____
_____

4. John 14:6. Finally, what did Christ teach to let the disciples and us know that we can only get to heaven through Him? _____
_____

The disciples were glad that Christ would be going to prepare a place for them in heaven. But after His death, the disciples still did not understand what would happen. They felt that they needed Christ even more than you feel you need your father. What would they do without Him? To comfort them, Christ had promised in John 14:18 not to leave them alone. The words Jesus used here mean, "as orphans, without any parents to look after you."

Christ had been like a father to the disciples—helping, guiding, and comforting them. Now He told them of a wonderful way in which He would continue to do these things for them, even when He would be in heaven. As we have learned, the Holy Spirit would take His place on the earth and actually live in the hearts of believers.

 According to John 14:16, how long would the Holy Spirit stay with them? _____

When Did The Holy Spirit Come?

 In John 16:7, Christ explained again how important it was for Him to go to heaven to be with the Father. What was the reason He gave? _____

_____

 Now read Acts 1:8–11. There were two promises made in these verses. Explain these promises below.

Promise #1 (made by Christ)	Promise #2 (made by the angels)

66

The word "Pentecost" refers to the fiftieth day. Christ ascended into heaven forty days after the resurrection. Ten days later the Holy Spirit came to earth on the Day of Pentecost. Read about this important event in Acts 2:1–4.

1. Who was there? (Note also Acts 1:15.) _____

2. Who filled them at this time? _____

3. What two things happened at that time that showed the power of God?

   a. _____

   b. _____

God In Us

It is very important for you to fully understand that when you are saved, a person comes to live within your body. This person is God Himself!

4. Read 1 Corinthians 14:25 and write down what it says about God's presence.

_____

_____

God is a person with a mind, will, and emotions.

- While you have some knowledge, God knows all things.
- While you have a desire to do right, God is perfectly righteous and never makes mistakes.
- While you have feelings that are often wrong, God always has a right attitude.

The God who has all knowledge and all power lives within those who are saved in the person of the Holy Spirit!

A. Now read 1 Corinthians 6:19 and explain in your own words what the verse says about who owns and lives in your body.

_____

_____

_____

This is why a Christian will have a changed life. He has God living in him, and God can give him greater wisdom, better attitudes, and the power to do right.

Building Your Life Castle

B. Remember: The Holy Spirit is a Helper, a Counselor, and a Comfort to Christians. To remind you of these truths, read John 14:26 and 16:13 and then match the statements below concerning what the Spirit's special ministry was to the apostles. These also give us clues as to how the Spirit can help us in our lives.

The Holy Spirit would...

1.		1. Teach them...	**A.**	...things to come.
2.		2. Help them remember...	**B.**	...all things.
3.		3. Guide them into...	**C.**	...what Jesus had said.
4.		4. Show them...	**D.**	...all truth.

5. If you are saved, tell how the Holy Spirit has been your Helper, Counselor, or Comforter.

_____

_____

_____

_____

LESSON 16
The Fruit Of The Spirit

VOCABULARY

Christ's Character Formed In Me

The personality and character of Jesus Christ is given to us through the Holy Spirit when He comes to live within us. Just as healthy fruit trees produce good fruit, a Christian should naturally have the right kind of spiritual fruit being produced inside because of the Holy Spirit.

✎ On the chart below, list the ninefold fruit of the Spirit in the order you find them in Galatians 5:22–23. When written in the proper order, they will match the definitions given in the right-hand column.

Fruit of the Spirit	Definition
1.	Letting God use me to help others
2.	True inner happiness based upon what God has done for me
3.	Contentment with my circumstances
4.	Patiently waiting upon the Lord
5.	Treating others as I would want to be treated
6.	Showing godliness in the way I act
7.	Being dependable because of my faith in God
8.	Humbly accepting whatever God brings in to my life
9.	Giving control of myself to the Holy Spirit

69

Puzzle

Write the words listed below in the following puzzle: (hint: start by filling in the word with the greatest number of letters).

| Love | Joy | Peace | Patience | Kindness |

| Goodness | Faithfulness | Gentleness | Self-control |

Are You Producing Spiritual Fruit?

The nine-part fruit of the Holy Spirit listed in Galatians 5:22–23 can give you a continuous test to see if you are letting God build His character in you. If the Spirit is producing this fruit in your life, these things will begin to show up in your actions and attitudes. If you have opposite traits in your character, you will know that He is not in control.

✏ In the first column, write each part of the fruit of the Spirit. In the second column, write one or two traits that would be the opposite of the trait you named.

Fruit of the Spirit	Opposite character traits
1. a	b
2. a	b
3. a	b
4. a	b
5. a	b
6. a	b
7. a	b
8. a	b
9. a	b

Building Your Life Castle

For each of the character qualities below, think of a way in which your life would be different if that quality were always a part of your life.

1	Love	
2	Joy	
3	Peace	
4	Patience	
5	Kindness	
6	Goodness	
7	Faithfulness	
8	Gentleness	
9	Self-control	

LESSON 17
Who Controls Your Life?

VOCABULARY

When Self Is In Control

✏️ In Genesis 27, you will find the story of the stolen blessing. Read the story and find out what happens when the Holy Spirit is not allowed to have control of your life. Jealousy, cheating, lying, anger, hurt feelings, bitterness, and many other sins can take control of your life if self becomes too important. Notice what happens when self is in control.

Genesis	What happened?	What sins are evident?
1. 27:6–10	What was Rebekah's plan? _____	b
2. 27:14–17	How did she plan to trick Isaac? _____	b
3. 27:28–30	Did the plan succeed? _____	b
4. 27:34–41	What was Esau's response? _____	b

5. ✏️ Now read Genesis 33:1–4. What happened when these same brothers met again many years later? _____

_____.

73

It is easy to understand Esau's attitude of bitterness and hatred when he found out what his mother had done. Because of this, Jacob left his home for over twenty years. During this time, the Lord worked in the hearts of both Jacob and Esau. They had allowed God to change their hearts. This is why their attitudes had changed when they saw each other again years later.

It is one thing to know what kind of person you ought to be. It is quite another to be that kind of person. But the Holy Spirit can help if you submit to Him.

What To Do When You Sin

A In Bible days, it was considered polite for a host to wash the feet of house guests who came in from the dusty streets. Christ used this gesture of kindness to teach His disciples an important lesson. Find this story in John 13.

1. What did Christ do (vs. 4–5)? _____

2. Which disciple did not want Him to wash his feet at first? (vs. 8) _____

3. Why did he feel this way? _____

4. For what reasons did Christ wash His disciples feet?

B
1. Read verse 15. Jesus wanted to provide them with an _____ of what it means to serve others.

2. Jesus wanted to teach them that they needed to be cleansed spiritually. Jesus was teaching that his followers needed to seek the cleansing from sin that He alone could provide.

Read 1 John 1:9. A person who really knows Christ as his Savior hates sin. Every true Christian wants to let the Lord clean up every part of him. Our hearts are perfectly clean when Christ saves us. But every day we are tempted to sin. The part of us that still enjoys sin wants to have control of our lives. When we sin, we feel guilty for our actions. That is why we need to confess our sins to the Lord in prayer and know that the Holy Spirit who lives within us will help us keep the sin out of our lives.

Your part

A. You must repent of your sin. This means that you agree with God that your sin displeases Him and that you want to turn to God from your sin.

According to 1 John 1:9, you must _____.

God's part

God is faithful and fair to do His part. From 1 John 1:9, what is God's part?

2. _____ our sins

3. _____ us from all unrighteousness

Building Your Life Castle

B. Who controls your life? Is it yourself or the Holy Spirit who is in control of you when you have the following attitudes?

1		"Why should I be kind to others if they haven't treated me kindly?"
2		"I'm glad I finished my homework early. It feels good to have it done."
3		"What difference does a little lie make? I haven't hurt anyone."
4		"I study the Bible in school all week so it doesn't matter if I miss Sunday school."
5		"Thank you, Lord for forgiving my sins."
6		"Brothers and sisters are really pests. They ruin everything!"
7		"I have some extra time. Is there something I can help you with?"
8		"It's not fair that you get a new pair of shoes. I have to wear the same old ones."
9		"Let's play ball. You can have your turn first."
10		"The Lord doesn't really care about me. He let me lose the game."
11		"I'm so glad you got a new dress. It looks so pretty on you."
12		"What's wrong with using bad language once in a while? All the other kids do it."

C. When you recognize that you have the wrong attitudes and feelings inside, what should you do? _____

_____

_____

LESSON 18
Having Confidence In The Lord

VOCABULARY

Mr. and Mrs. Harold Taylor were missionaries to West China in 1941. They were anxious to come home to San Francisco so they asked for reservations on a ship destined for America. They tried and tried to get their reservations but could not get a place on the ship.

Later, they tried to get reservations on another ship. This time their request was granted, and they arrived safely in San Francisco.

One week later, the Japanese attacked Pearl Harbor. The ship they had wanted to take, the *USS President Harrison*, fell into the hands of the Japanese. The ship never reached San Francisco. Then the Taylors could understand and were thankful to God for not allowing them to go on the ship they had first tried to get on.

The Taylors had learned to have confidence in God. They knew that God would listen to their prayers and do what was best for them. They knew that when God says no, He has a good reason. We may not always be able to see the reason as clearly or as soon as the Taylors did, but we can be sure that God will always answer our prayers in the right way.

1. What does the word "confidence" mean? _____

_____

_____

2. What then does it mean to have "confidence in the Lord"? _____

_____

_____

Conditions For Answered Prayer

✏️ Read the verses on the chart below and list some conditions we must meet in order to have our prayers answered. When we can understand how God thinks and acts, then we can learn to have more confidence in Him and His decisions concerning us.

	Verses	Conditions for answered prayer
1	1 John 3:22	
2	1 John 5:14–15	
3	Psalm 37:4	

Trusting In God's Promises

God wants us to learn to have confidence in Him. When we pray and begin to see how God answers our prayers, we will learn to trust Him more.

When you read the previous verses and saw conditions for having your prayers answered, you saw that God has commands for us to follow. We need to learn to obey God's commands so that we will show He is more important than anything else in our lives. We also need to learn that when God gives us a command, He often has a wonderful promise for us.

 In each of the verses below, you will see both a command and a promise.

	Verses	God's command	God's promise
1	Psalm 34:9	a.	b.
2	Psalm 37:4	a.	b.
3	Ephesians 6:1–3	a.	b.
4	Hebrews 13:5	a.	b.
5	James 4:7	a.	b.

Confidence For Eternity

A. God wants us to learn to have confidence in Him. He wants us to know that He hears and answers our prayers. He wants us to know that He has many promises for our lives. But the most important thing He wants us to understand is that we can live with Him forever.

1. Read 1 John 5:11–13. According to these verses, how can we know that we have eternal life?

   _____
   _____

2. Does eternal life ever end? _____

3. Read Hebrews 13:8. What three words from this verse describe how long eternal life lasts?

   a. 1. _____
   b. 2. _____
   c. 3. _____

B. The greatest truth you will ever learn in your life is that by believing in Jesus Christ, you can know for sure that you will have eternal life in heaven. God wants us to have confidence in the knowledge of this fact. Over and over again in His Word, He teaches us this truth.

1. Now let's look at how God brings out this truth in 1, 2, and 3 John. These books were all written about A.D. 90 by the Apostle _____. First John has _____ chapters. Second and Third John each have only _____ chapter.

2. First John 5:11 says that God has given us _____ life, and this life is in His Son.

3. In 3 John 12, the Apostle John makes sure we understand that this testimony is _____. God cannot lie.

79

1. Then 2 John 1 and 2 tell us that the truth lives (dwells) _____ us if we believe, and it will be with us _____.

2. Remember that the truth of God does not change. Jesus Christ is the same _____, _____, and _____ (Hebrews 13:8).

Building Your Life Castle

3. God's Word will never change. God does not change His mind as man sometimes will do. When He makes a promise, He will keep His promise because God cannot lie. We studied in this lesson about some of the promises of God. Think about which of God's promises mean the most to you and write them below.

_____
_____
_____
_____
_____
_____
_____
_____

LESSON 19
God's Concern For You

VOCABULARY

Every Detail Planned By God

A Do you think you just happened to be born? Are your looks and your abilities and talents just an accident? God says that He knew all about you before you were born. He planned which family you would be a part of. He planned what you would look like. He carefully planned a wonderful life for you.

1. Read Psalm 139:14 and explain why you should praise God. _____
   _____

2. God designed every part of you and your life—your appearance, your family, and your special talents and abilities. God also designed you so that certain things would be difficult for you to do. Think this through and then write beside each area listed below what you can understand about how God decided to design you.

   a. My appearance: _____
   _____

   b. My family: _____
   _____

   c. My special abilities and talents: _____
   _____

   d. Things that are difficult for me to do: _____
   _____

81

A. Now let's read from Psalm 139. Read the following verses and fill in the blanks.

1. Psalm 139:2—God knows my _____ from far away.

2. Psalm 139:4—He knows every _____ I say.

3. Psalm 139:10—His _____ leads me.

4. Psalm 139:11—I might say that darkness could _____ me.

5. Psalm 139:12—Night is the same as _____ to God, and _____ is like light to Him.

B. The rest of Psalm 139 explains in even more detail that God definitely planned you and knew all about you before you were born. Read Psalm 139:13–18 and fill in the blanks.

1. Psalm 139:14—I will _____ you because I am…wonderfully made.

2. Psalm 139:16—God's _____ saw what I was made of before I was formed.

3. Psalm 139:17—Your _____ are precious to me, O God!

4. Psalm 139:18—When I _____, I am still with you.

Thanking God For His Perfect Plan

When we wish we could look differently, when we wish we were able to do something that is difficult for us but easy for someone else, or when we wish we had an ability or talent that God has given to another, we are forgetting to thank God for His thoughtfulness to us. We are forgetting to think about the positive things God has given us for our lives. We need to thank Him for the thoughtful way He has made us.

We must remember that God designed us for a purpose, and sometimes we do not immediately see His purpose for us.

1. Read Isaiah 55:9 and explain in your own words what it means. _____

_____

_____

_____

God's plan and thoughts for your life are greater than you can imagine. He wants to show you His perfect plan for your life. Since He made you and planned all things, you now need to learn to trust Him to make your life what it should be. Never settle for less than God's best!

Building Your Life Castle

2. After thinking about the ideas in this lesson, read 1 Peter 5:6–7. In your own words, explain what these verses tell you to do. If there are things that you have wished were different about you, list those things here also. Then give your concern about them to God and let Him show you His purpose for your life.

_____

_____

_____

_____

_____

_____

_____

_____

LESSON 20
Your Inner Character

VOCABULARY

We have seen that God has taken care to design your appearance, your abilities, your family, and many other things about you. But these are all external areas of your life. In other words, these are the areas of your life that other people can see. These external areas are complete—they cannot be changed very much. You can work hard to use your abilities and talents to glorify God and do your best, but you cannot change what you are externally.

But there is another part of you that is not yet complete. This is the inside or internal part of you. It has been said that the end result of education is the development of character. Character is not developed externally but rather internally, or inside you. This is the area God wants to help you change and develop. God is most interested in your growing up "on the inside."

Internal Character Development

 There are many traits of Christian character that God is trying to develop internally—inside you! Some of these traits are named in the puzzle below. The main idea of thinking about these traits is to begin to let God develop them in your life.

God wants us to be...

1	Matthew 5:7		C	
2	James 4:10		H	
3	Revelation 2:10		A	
4	Matthew 5:8		R	
5	Ephesians 4:32		A	
6	1 Timothy 6:8		C	
7	1 Peter 1:14		T	
8	2 Peter 3:14		E	
9	Matthew 5:9		R	

Conformed To Christ's Image

B. God has a plan for developing our character. Read Romans 8:28–29. In the following blanks, write the truths from these verses to help you better understand God's plan:

- God says that all things work together for good for those who…

    1. _____.

    2. _____.

- Then God says that He knew beforehand and has planned for us to be _____

    to the image of His Son.

This means that God wants to make our character conform to the character of Jesus Christ. He wants us to learn to be more and more like Christ. When we studied Christ's life, we saw how He acted. One reason Christ came to earth was to give us an example of what we are to become. Now that the Holy Spirit lives in us as Christians, the Holy Spirit will teach us and help us to be more like Christ. Then we will become "conformed to His image."

The Beatitudes

✏️ On the following chart, list each Christ-like attitude that should be a part of our lives and then write the specific promise that is made to those whose attitudes are like Christ's in that specific way.

	Christ-like attitude	Matthew	Promise
1		5:3	
2		5:4	
3		5:5	
4		5:6	
5		5:7	
6		5:8	
7		5:9	
8		5:10	

Building Your Life Castle

✏️ We have listed many of the character qualities that God wants to develop in your life. Look over the things you have written during this lesson. As you look over the list, think of which areas you have already developed in your character and write these below. Then find some areas that need to become a part of your life and list these also. These are the areas God wants to begin to work on in your life.

	Christ-like attitudes that are already a part of my life	Christ-like attitudes that I need to develop
1		
2		
3		
4		
5		

✏️ Are you willing to allow God to develop His character in you in all that you do? _____

Lesson 21
Humility: Doing Things God's Way

VOCABULARY

_____
_____
_____
_____

In the last lesson, we studied the Beatitudes. The first Beatitude is directed to the "poor in spirit." "Poor in spirit" means to be humble. Humility means to let God have His rightful place in your life. It means that we understand how big God is and how small we are. Remember that God designed us for a special purpose and has a wonderful plan for us. Also remember that God's care and concern for us are far beyond anything we can imagine or understand. It is only reasonable to give Him first place in our lives so He will be glorified through our lives.

1. What is the meaning of the word "pride"? _____
_____

2. If you have too much pride, are you usually doing things your own way or God's way?
_____

3. Why do you think God wants you to be "poor in spirit"? _____
_____
_____

God's Design For David

We know that God knew what you would be like even before you were born. He chose the right parents for you. He decided what you should look like. And He has a plan for your life.

Read 1 Samuel 16:1–13 in your Bible. Here God begins the story of the life of David. Find out about the life and family God designed for David.

1. How did God design David to look? (vs. 12)_____

2. Describe the family God gave David. _____
_____.

3. What work (job) did God give to David while he was young? _____

4. What was God's plan for David's future?_____
_____

5. According to 1 Samuel 16:7, what is the difference between the way man sees things and the way God sees things?_____
_____

The Ways Of Man Vs. The Ways Of God

The ways of man tell us that we should be proud, but the ways of God tell us that we should be humble. Completing the following two puzzles will help you understand more about the differences between the ways of man and the ways of God.

Read the following verses to complete the puzzle. Then unscramble the letters in the light green boxes to find out the result of following the ways of man.

1. Man's ways lead to _____ (Matthew 7:13).
2. The ways of evil people are _____ (Proverbs 2:12–13).
3. Destruction and _____ are in man's ways (Romans 3:16).
4. The Bible calls man's ways _____ (Proverbs 2:15).

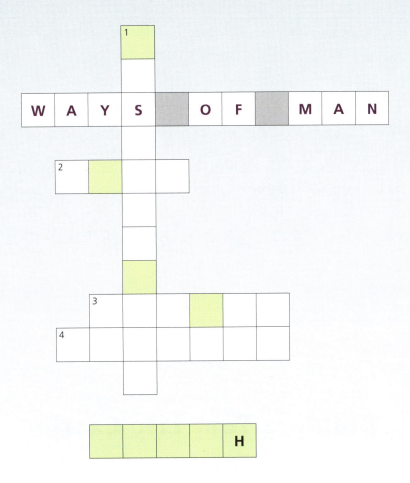

Read the following verses to complete the puzzle. Then unscramble the highlighted letters to find out the result of following the ways of God.

1. God's way is _____ (Psalm 18:30).
2. David wanted God to lead him in the _____ way (Psalm 139:24).
3. All who walk in God's ways are _____ (Psalm 128:1).
4. God's ways are _____ and true (Revelation 15:3).
5. The ways of the Lord are _____ (Hosea 14:9).
6. God's ways are _____ than our ways (Isaiah 55:9).

WAYS OF GOD

____ E

Building Your Life Castle

What part of you is God most interested in? _____

Why do you think it is important to be humble before God and to desire to do things God's way? _____

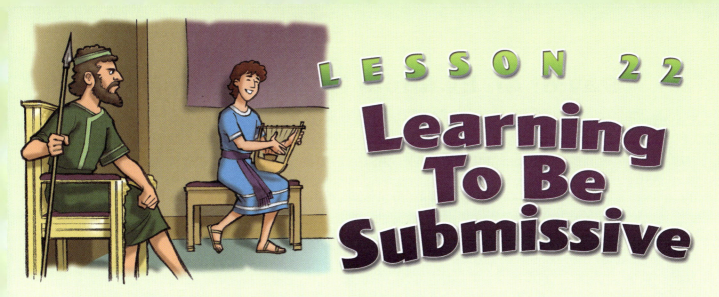

VOCABULARY

Submitting To Authority

Before you can be used by God, you will need to learn to obey those God has placed over you. It is part of God's design for your life that you have parents and teachers and other leaders to help you in your life. It is important to learn to obey and respect these people in order for God to work in your life.

 Read the verses listed below and fill in the chart to learn about the leaders God has placed in your life and how God wants you to act toward them.

	Verses	God gave you these leaders	How you are to treat those in authority
1	Exodus 20:12 Ephesians 6:1–2	a	b
2	Proverbs 5:13	a	b
3	1 Timothy 2:1–2	a	b

4. Why does God desire that you respect those in authority over you? See Ephesians 6:3 and 1 Timothy 2:2. _____

_____

_____

David: An Example Of Submission

In your last lesson, you learned that God had chosen David to be king of Israel. God did this when David was a young boy. But it was to be a long time before David could really become the king.

This was a very important position. To be the right kind of king, David would have to learn many lessons. God had chosen David to be the king, but He still had lessons for David to learn. One of these lessons was always to have the right attitude toward those in authority.

After David killed Goliath, Saul watched how the people admired and respected David. King Saul became jealous of the feelings the people had for David. Saul's jealousy turned into hatred for David. Soon the hatred made Saul want to kill David. Now David began to run from Saul in fear of his life. Saul was determined that David would be killed.

Read 1 Samuel 19:1–18 and check the correct answers below.

1. Who warned David of King Saul's plan to murder him? (vs. 2)
   - [ ] Saul's servants
   - [ ] Saul's son

2. Who promised Jonathan that David would not be killed? (vs. 6)
   - [ ] Saul
   - [ ] Samuel
   - [ ] The Lord

3. When war broke out again, what did David do to the Philistines? (vs. 8)
   - [ ] Joined them
   - [ ] Killed them

4. With what weapon did Saul try to kill David? (vs. 10)
   - [ ] Javelin or spear
   - [ ] Knife
   - [ ] Stones

5. Who helped David escape through a window that night? (vs. 12)
   - [ ] Michal
   - [ ] An angel
   - [ ] Nobody

6. What did David's wife tell Saul's men when they came to take David? (vs. 14)
   - [ ] "He's sick."
   - [ ] "He's dead."
   - [ ] "He left."

David had to flee in similar ways from Saul again and again. Each time Saul learned where David had gone, he called his men together and tried to kill David. During all of these experiences, God was teaching David the lessons he needed to learn before he could become king

Building Your Life Castle

Think about your own relationships with others. David had a situation to deal with that was worse than anything you will probably ever face. God wants you to learn to respond properly in every area of your life.

 Check yourself in the areas below to see where you stand.

With yourself and God

#			
1	☐ Yes	☐ No	Are you trusting Jesus Christ to be your Savior?
2	☐ Yes	☐ No	Do you listen to God's Word in Bible class and church so that you can become more godly?
3	☐ Yes	☐ No	Are you grateful to God for the things He has provided for you?
4	☐ Yes	☐ No	Do you really try to do your best work at school?
5	☐ Yes	☐ No	Do you choose friends that will help you to become more godly because they encourage you to obey and be thankful?
6	☐ Yes	☐ No	Do you praise God during the day and thank Him for His gifts?

With your parents

#			
7	☐ Yes	☐ No	Do you willingly listen to the advice and direction from your parents?
8	☐ Yes	☐ No	Do you willingly obey them when they ask you to do something?
9	☐ Yes	☐ No	Do you consistently do your chores without being told?
10	☐ Yes	☐ No	Do you make sure you do not talk back or argue with them?
11	☐ Yes	☐ No	Do you try to do things for your parents to make them happy?

With your family

☐ Yes	☐ No	Do you honestly try to be pleasant around your house?
☐ Yes	☐ No	Do you take time to play and share with and help your brothers and sisters?
☐ Yes	☐ No	Are you unselfish with your brothers and sisters?
☐ Yes	☐ No	Are you careful not to begin fights?
☐ Yes	☐ No	Do you honestly try to help make your home a peaceful, pleasant, and fun place to live?

LESSON 23
Learning To Obey

VOCABULARY

Christ Obeyed His Father

✏️ The Lord Jesus knew how to obey. He was willing to obey in all things because He knew God would always do what was best. Finish the following sentences and think about what Christ had to do to obey His Father.

1. Christ took on Himself the form of a _____ (Philippians 2:7).

2. Christ came to _____ the Scriptures (John 19:36).

3. Christ died to give us eternal _____ (John 3:16).

4. Christ set an _____ for us (1 Peter 2:21).

5. We should give _____ to God in everything (1 Thessalonians 5:18).

Learning To Be A Leader

✏️ God had placed David under the authority of King Saul. Saul was jealous of David and hated him so much that he wanted him dead. Why do you think God allowed David to wait under such an authority before He made him king?

_____
_____
_____

Finally, God allowed something to happen that showed David's true character. Saul, along with 3,000 soldiers, came looking for David. They came to a cave, and Saul decided to take a rest. He lay down inside the cave and went to sleep. He had no idea that David and his men were also inside the cave watching his every move. Read 1 Samuel 24 and answer the following questions about what happened:

1. When David's men saw what was happening, they thought David should kill Saul while he had the chance. Instead, what did David do (vs. 4)? _____

_____

2. Why didn't he kill Saul (vs. 6)? _____

_____

3. When Saul woke up and left the cave, David followed him. David asked why Saul believed those who said David was trying to harm him. What did David show Saul then? (vs. 11)

_____

4. What does this story tell you about the character of David? How do you know that he was learning the lessons God had been teaching him? _____

_____

_____

_____

Learning To Be Patient

✏️ One of the greatest lessons God was teaching David was to learn to be patient. David had to face very difficult times while waiting to become king. But God had reasons for letting these things happen. David had to learn patience and understanding and to have faith in God. God wants you to learn the same lessons.

1. We can be strengthened in our inner being by God's _____ (Ephesians 3:16).

2. We get spiritual strength by learning to _____ _____ the Lord (Isaiah 40:31).

3. When I feel weak, then I can really be _____ by trusting in the Lord (2 Corinthians 12:10).

4. Patient endurance results when God tests our _____ (James 1:3).

5. By going through times of trouble we learn to _____ God's Word more (Psalm 119:67).

6. Things may seem difficult, but we do get help from God's _____ (Hebrews 12:11).

7. Christ said that we have _____ in Him (John 16:33).

8. Through faith and patience we can inherit God's _____ (Hebrews 6:12).

Building Your Life Castle

B. ✏️ In what way was Christ our example in being willing to obey? _____
_____

2. ✏️ David had to learn to obey and be patient while he waited on God. Think of some times in your own life in which you need to learn to obey and be patient.

   a. _____

   b. _____

   c. _____

✏️ Why should you be willing to obey in all things? _____
_____
_____

LESSON 24
Learning To Trust God

VOCABULARY

The chart below is a picture of different aspects of your life that the Lord wants you to give over to Him. When we trust God to provide for our needs in these areas, then God will work things out for our best. But we must remember to accept responsibility for each area, even though God will take care of all of these things. A student cannot say, "God will take care of my grades, so I do not have to study anymore." We still have the responsibility to follow through in many different ways.

✏ Read each verse and then choose from the list which area God is discussing in the verse.

Word List

| Future | Needs | Self | Possessions | Friends | Clothes |

1	1 Peter 3:3–4	
2	Luke 15:31	
3	Matthew 10:39	
4	Philippians 4:19	
5	Mark 14:36	
6	Proverbs 18:24	

✏️ Use the verses to fill in the chart below. After reading the verses, explain in your own words how God wants you to think in each area. Then explain what responsibility you must still accept for that area.

Verse List

| 1 Peter 3:3–4 | Luke 15:31 | Matthew 10:39 | Philippians 4:19 | Mark 14:36 | Proverbs 18:24 |

Area	Verse	How God wants me to think	My responsibility
1. Self			
2. Clothes			
3. Needs			
4. Possessions			
5. Friends			
6. Future			

George Mueller: A Man Of Faith

Over 200 years ago in England lived a man named George Mueller. He was a frail little man, so he looked like a weak person. But he had strong faith in God. As you read the following story about his life, you will see how Mr. Mueller truly trusted God in every area we discussed above.

George Mueller was a preacher with very little money, but he liked to help people. He saw hundreds of children in the streets of his city who had no fathers or mothers to give them homes, food, clothing, or love.

Mr. Mueller wanted to start an orphanage for these children. The more he prayed about it, the more he felt sure that it was the right way for him to serve God.

Along with his decision to start an orphanage, he made an even more important decision to trust God. He knew he would need food, lodging, and many other things for the orphans. "I will not ask other people for any offerings," he thought. "I will pray and ask God to give what I need for the orphanage. If I ask people, I may come to depend on them. I want to see what God alone can do."

So Mr. Mueller held a public meeting and told people he was starting a home for orphans. But he did not mention money. At this time, he had less than fifty cents! He prayed and then rented a building. Within one month he was taking care of twenty-six children. The money came in for food and clothes and buildings. He never turned an orphan away.

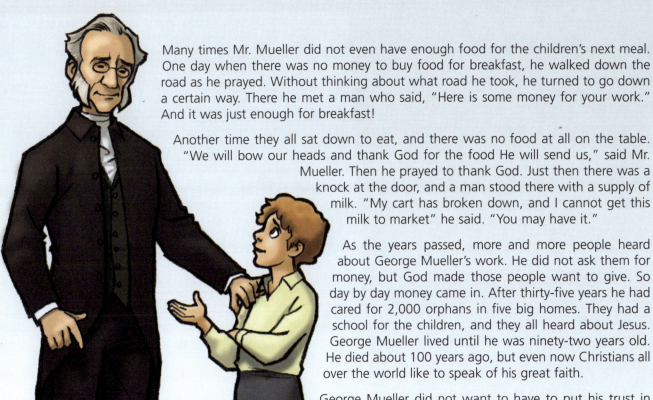

Many times Mr. Mueller did not even have enough food for the children's next meal. One day when there was no money to buy food for breakfast, he walked down the road as he prayed. Without thinking about what road he took, he turned to go down a certain way. There he met a man who said, "Here is some money for your work." And it was just enough for breakfast!

Another time they all sat down to eat, and there was no food at all on the table. "We will bow our heads and thank God for the food He will send us," said Mr. Mueller. Then he prayed to thank God. Just then there was a knock at the door, and a man stood there with a supply of milk. "My cart has broken down, and I cannot get this milk to market" he said. "You may have it."

As the years passed, more and more people heard about George Mueller's work. He did not ask them for money, but God made those people want to give. So day by day money came in. After thirty-five years he had cared for 2,000 orphans in five big homes. They had a school for the children, and they all heard about Jesus. George Mueller lived until he was ninety-two years old. He died about 100 years ago, but even now Christians all over the world like to speak of his great faith.

George Mueller did not want to have to put his trust in people. That is why he would never ask people for help or money. He wanted to see God supply him with everything he needed.

George Mueller gave his life and all his possessions to God. He kept nothing back to worry about because he knew God could solve every problem. It was fun for him to watch God work. You can learn to have the same kind of faith because God is interested in you just as much as He was in George Mueller.

Our Faith In God

The following verses all talk about having faith in God. Add the missing words in the sentences.

1. Romans 10:17—_____ comes by hearing God's Word about Christ.

2. Ephesians 6:16—With the _____ of _____ we are able to quench all the fiery arrows of the wicked one.

3. 1 Timothy 6:12—We fight the _____ _____ of faith.

4. Hebrews 11:1—Faith is being sure of what we _____ for.

5. Hebrews 12:2—We look to _____, the Author and Finisher of our faith, who endured the cross, despising its shame.

LESSON 25
A Forgiving Spirit

VOCABULARY

Being Merciful To Our Enemies

When others hurt us in any way, it is difficult to respond in the right way. Usually our attitude is to return hurt in the same way. Often we think that we will forgive people if they ask for forgiveness and admit that what they did was wrong. Christ taught us a different way to respond. We need to learn to forgive no matter what the other person thinks or feels.

We need to forgive because it is best for us. If we hold a grudge or have hatred or anger within us, then we are hurting ourselves. God wants us to have peace inside, not resentment.

✏️ Read the following two Beatitudes from Matthew 5 and answer these questions:

1. Verse 7: What is the reward for the merciful? _____
_____
_____

2. What does the word "merciful" mean? _____
_____
_____

3. Verse 9: What is the reward for the peacemakers? _____
_____
_____

✏️ Now read Luke 6:27–31 and tell in your own words how God wants you to learn to respond to the following people:

Problem	Response
My enemies	
Those who hate me	
Those who curse me	
Those who treat me wrongly	

David: An Example Of Forgiveness

No one had more reason to hate someone than David did. But "getting even" with someone is never the answer. David passed up two chances to kill King Saul. Both times Saul was trying to kill David. David truly had a forgiving spirit.

Read 2 Samuel 1:1–16. In this story, an Amalekite told David that Saul was dead. To prove it, he gave David Saul's bracelet and crown. This Amalekite said he had killed the king (see vs. 10).

 Many men would have been glad to hear such news after all Saul had done. Read verses 11 and 12 and write how David really felt about Saul's death.

_____

_____

_____

In 2 Samuel 2:4, David is crowned king. In the long years that David had waited to become king, he had learned many important lessons.

 Tell how you think David showed that he had the following character traits:

A forgiving spirit	
Patience	
Humility	

106

Using God's Eyes

✏️ God is trying to teach us to look at people from His point of view rather than through our own eyes. Look up the following verses and find out what God is trying to teach you:

- Ephesians 4:32. What should be our example for forgiving others? _____
  _____

- Matthew 18:21–22. How many times should you forgive someone who wrongs you?
  _____
  _____

- Luke 23:34. Christ could have become very bitter toward those who beat Him and nailed Him to the cross. What was His real attitude? _____
  _____
  _____

- Colossians 3:13. How does this verse teach that Christ is our example? _____
  _____
  _____

Important Character Qualities

✏️ Unscramble the character qualities to complete the following sentences:

- You have to have _____ to believe that God can do what is best.
  afhit

- David had _____ on King Saul.
  naspomcsio

- We should be _____ for all things.
  fulhatnk

- Solomon was full of knowledge and _____.
  idsomw

- We need to have an attitude of _____ for those who hurt us.
  rgifvnsseeo

- Christ bore the cross of shame, rejection, and _____.
  ulihyimt

- David showed _____ for all the Lord asked him to do.
  ediecnebo

Building Your Life Castle

1. Read Luke 6:32–34 and tell in your own words what Christ is trying to make you understand.
   _____
   _____
   _____

2. Now read verse 35 and write what God promises to those who obey Him in this area.
   _____
   _____

3. Is there someone right now who has hurt your feelings or made you upset and angry? _____

4. Is there someone whom you need to forgive? _____

5. What attitude does God want you to learn to have? _____
   _____
   _____
   _____

LESSON 26
Making Wise Choices

VOCABULARY

Knowledge, Wisdom, And Understanding

✏️ Most people do not really understand the differences among the words "knowledge," "wisdom," and "understanding." Write out and learn the definitions for these three important words.

1. Knowledge: _____
   _____

2. Wisdom: _____
   _____

3. Understanding: _____
   _____

No one likes to be called a fool. But many people are fools without even realizing it. The Bible calls them fools because they reject the truth of God. They do not have true wisdom and understanding that can only come from God. The Bible says that the fear of the Lord is the beginning of knowledge (Proverbs 1:7). "The fear of the Lord" means that we are to have a great respect and trust for God. It does not mean we are to be scared of Him.

A

1. Now read Job 28:28. What did God say is wisdom? _____

_____

2. What did God say about how we demonstrate understanding? _____

_____

God's Word is clear. Wisdom and understanding are from God.

Christ's Parable On Wisdom

In Matthew 7:24–27, Christ gave a lesson to teach us how to live our lives. Learning should change us and make us wiser. Allow the knowledge of this story to give you more wisdom and understanding for your own life.

3. In verse 24, Christ says we are to a. _____ His words and then b. _____ them in order to be wise. To do this we must build our lives on the c. _____ (Jesus Christ). In verse 26, Christ shows us that a fool d. _____ His words but does not e. _____ them. A fool does not build his life on anything lasting and solid. He builds on f. _____ .

The Foolish Man Vs. The Wise Man

B The following verses have to do with the foolish man and the wise man. Read each verse and write how each says that these two men are different.

Proverbs	The foolish man	The wise man
1. 1:7	a.	b.
2. 12:23	a.	b.
3. 14:9	a.	b.
4. 15:2	a.	b.
5. 15:5	a.	b.

✏️ How can you have wisdom and understanding? Read the following verses to find out:

1. Proverbs 1:8–10 _____

   _____

2. Proverbs 3:5–6 _____

   _____

The Wisest Man Who Ever Lived

✏️ Read the story of King Solomon in 1 Kings 3:5–14. It has been written that Solomon was the wisest man in the Bible. In this story you will see why this was true.

1. Verse 7. How did Solomon see himself? Did he think he was wise?

2. Verse 9. What did Solomon ask from the Lord?

3. Verse 11. God noticed that Solomon had not asked for certain things. What were those?

4. Verses 12–13. God gave Solomon what he requested. He also gave him those things that he had not requested. What were those things?

5. Verse 14. What does God want us to do?

Building Your Life Castle

A. What would be some wise and foolish choices that you might have to make in each of the following areas?

		Foolish choice	Wise choice
1	I want to get a good grade on a test.	a.	b.
2	I want to be friends, but my friend wants to do wrong.	a.	b.
3	I'm supposed to be home at a certain time, but I'm having a good time.	a.	b.

B. As a review, write the definitions for the following three words:

1. Knowledge: _____

2. Wisdom: _____
   _____

3. Understanding: _____
   _____

C. In your own words, explain the difference between a foolish man and a wise man.

_____
_____

LESSON 27
Compassion For Others

Learning To Get Along With Others

One of the main problems in life is getting along with people. Others can make us angry or hurt our feelings very easily. And we know that God does not want us to be angry or feel hurt inside. He wants us to learn how to have the right attitude toward others.

A. In the box below, match the two parts of each sentence by writing the letter of the part that completes the sentence.

1	When a child hits a friend,...	A.	...they can have good times.
2	When two people are friendly,...	B.	...to do what leads to peace with others.
3	We feel much better when...	C.	...but God helps them work together.
4	After you have a fight,...	D.	...the friend usually hits back.
5	You need to make every effort...	E.	...people are friendly to us.
6	People don't always agree,...	F.	...you feel sorry.

You know that God made you, He loves you, and He has a plan for your life. But this is exactly how God feels about everyone else also. When you are upset by someone else or think you are better than he is, you are forgetting that this person is as special and important to God as you are. God wants us to learn to treat everyone as we want to be treated.

B. This is why God has said that there are really only two commandments. If we learn to keep these two commandments, we will always treat others properly. Read Matthew 22:36–40. Write these two commandments below in your own words.

1. _____

_____

2. _____

_____

113

The Example Of The Good Samaritan

A ✏️ Some of these lessons were taught in a parable by Jesus. Read the parable of the Good Samaritan in Luke 10:30–37.

1. Why do you think the first two men passed the man by and left him to die? _____
   _____
   _____

2. Why would it probably be difficult for the Samaritan to want to stop and help the Jew?
   _____

3. In what way did the Samaritan do more than was even necessary to help the man in trouble? _____
   _____

B ✏️ The following verses will help you understand how God wants you to look at others. In your own words, tell what the verses say.

1. Proverbs 17:17 _____

2. Luke 6:27–28 _____
   _____

3. Mark 12:31 _____

Learning To Be Friendly

Which of these boys…	
1. Looks at others from God's point of view?	
2. Shows he is more concerned about himself?	
3. Is afraid when meeting new people?	
4. Is interested in others?	
5. Has many friends?	
6. Has trouble making new friends?	
7. Does not get his feelings hurt easily?	
8. Worries too much?	
9. Has too much pride?	
10. Truly wants to help others?	

Building Your Life Castle

A. How well do you keep the second of the great commandments—to love your neighbor as yourself? Use the following as a checklist and rate yourself:

		Good	Fair	Poor
1	Do I often think I am better than others?	☐	☐	☐
2	Do I share what I have?	☐	☐	☐
3	Do I show interest in others?	☐	☐	☐
4	Do I get my feelings hurt easily?	☐	☐	☐
5	Do I try to help others?	☐	☐	☐
6	Do I worry about what others think of me?	☐	☐	☐
7	Do I love others as God does?	☐	☐	☐

B. In what ways do you think the Lord is showing you the need to change your attitude toward others? _____

_____

_____

_____

_____

_____

LESSON 28
Courage To Stand Alone

VOCABULARY

What a person is on the inside is the most important thing about him! Sincerity, honesty, unselfishness, intelligence, the spirit of cooperation and justice, cheerfulness, courtesy, concentration, and all the rest help make one what he is. What one is—that is character! Nothing else helps you stand the tests of life with all its dangers and problems like strong character.

Making Right Choices

Making right choices is part of standing alone. So many times we just go along with the crowd or do what our friends are doing, but God wants us to grow up and think before we act.

✏ Write the portion of each verse below that teaches the principle stated with it.

1. Life's most important choice is whom we will serve. Joshua 24:15:

   _____
   _____

2. Someone has to guide us in our choices. Proverbs 16:9:

   _____

3. Having a good name is a result of making right choices. Proverbs 22:1:

   _____
   _____

4. Some people choose not to follow Jesus Christ. Matthew 12:30:

   _____

117

🖉 Look at the principles and verses again and explain how you can make sure you are making the right choices for your own life.

_____

_____

_____

Daniel: A Man Of Courage

The Book of Daniel is full of examples showing the courage of a young person to stand alone for what is right. Daniel was a young man in a strange land. His parents were not with him. He was alone with two or three friends. It would have been easy to do things the rulers wanted him to do rather than follow God. Daniel had to make some important choices early in his life that would decide the kind of character that he would have for all his life.

By the time the events of Daniel 6 occurred, Daniel was an older man. The choices he made when he was young were still a part of his life. Instead of being a young slave boy, however, God had given Daniel responsibility as one of the leaders of this land. Some of the other rulers were trying to find fault with Daniel so they could get rid of him. They had the king make a new law in order to trap Daniel. Read the story in Daniel 6.

2.🖉 What law was made (vs. 7)? _____

_____

3.🖉 What was the punishment to be for anyone breaking the law? _____

_____

A

1. ✏️ Daniel could easily have prayed in silence behind closed doors to protect himself. What did he do instead (vs. 10)? _____

2. ✏️ Because he prayed, Daniel was thrown to the lions. How did God protect him (vs. 20–23? _____

3. ✏️ What kept Daniel from being hurt in any way (vs. 23)? _____

The story of Daniel is not fictional. Daniel was just as real as you are, and he loved the same God who loves you. God wants people to trust God today just like Daniel did in Bible times.

Building Your Life Castle

B All of us have the responsibility to make our character what it ought to be. The crucial choice lies in the little words "yes" and "no." Saying "yes" to all that life offers that is good and right, and saying "no" to all that can weaken or defile will form character that is strong, pure, and fine.

1. ✏️ In your own words, what is a person's character? _____

2. ✏️ Why is it so important to have the courage to say "no"? _____

3. ✏️ List areas in which God would want you to have the courage to stand alone. As you learn to say "no" in these areas, you will develop strong and godly character.

_____
_____
_____
_____
_____
_____
_____
_____

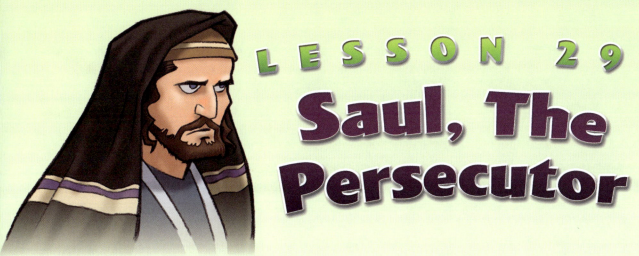

LESSON 29
Saul, The Persecutor

VOCABULARY

Let's review what we have studied this year. First, we studied the life of Christ. We saw how He was born and how He lived while He was on the earth. We learned about the purpose of His miracles. We studied His parables. We understood that His purpose for coming to the earth was to die on the cross in our place. We learned about the details of the crucifixion. Then we learned about His resurrection. We know that He was seen going into heaven where He now sits at the right hand of God. Then we learned that Christ sent the Holy Spirit to the earth to live inside the Christian. We have learned how the Holy Spirit works. We are beginning to understand how the Holy Spirit works in our lives.

After these things had happened, it was time for the gospel (or good news) of Jesus Christ to be taken to the world. For this to happen, God chose a man to carry this message. This man was the Apostle Paul, and it is his life and ministry that we will now study.

When we first meet Paul, we learn that he is not a Christian. He is a Jew who has been raised to hate Christians. Paul's Jewish name was Saul.

✎ Read Acts 8:3 and explain specifically what Saul was doing to Christians. _____

_____

_____

The First Christian Martyr

✎ The first time Saul is mentioned is as a witness at the stoning of the first Christian martyr. Look up the word "martyr" and write its meaning here. _____

_____

Stephen was martyred because he spoke out against the Jews' unbelief. Stephen was trying to teach these people about the gospel of Jesus Christ. Stephen wanted them to understand that Jesus Christ was the Messiah who had been promised to Adam, Abraham, David, and many other men throughout the Old Testament times. He wanted them to trust Jesus Christ as their Savior.

 Read Acts 7:54–60 and record below the actions and words of the following people:

	Acts	Person(s)	Actions or words used
1	7:54	Jews	
2	7:55	Stephen	
3	7:56	Stephen	
4	7:57	Jews	
5	7:58	Jews	
6	7:58	Saul	
7	7:59	Stephen	
8	7:59	Jews	
9	7:60	Stephen	
10	8:1	Saul	

We can be sure that Saul would always remember the day he watched Stephen being stoned because he was a Christian. Because Saul was a Jewish leader, he felt it was his duty to kill Christians. But still, he must have noticed Stephen's attitude and the things Stephen said when he was being stoned to death. There is only one way that Stephen could have had an attitude of forgiveness toward those who stoned him.

 This reason is found in Acts 7:55, where it says he was full of the _____

_____.

Jesus Christ gave us this same example when He was on the cross. And it is the Holy Spirit of God living in us that can give us the same peace in our hearts that Jesus had. This is why Stephen was able to have peace during tribulation.

Saul Continues His Persecution

Even with the example of Stephen before him, Saul continued to persecute Christians. Because of Saul, the Christians were forced to scatter into many cities to escape persecution. But even during persecution, God's Word cannot be stopped.

1. Did Saul's treatment of the Christians stop the spread of the gospel? _____

2. How did God use this situation for His glory (Acts 8:4)? _____
_____

3. Read Acts 9:1–2. Had Saul's attitude toward Christians changed? _____

4. What two things does verse 1 say Saul was doing?_____
_____

5. According to verse 2, what journey had Saul decided to make, and what was his purpose?
_____
_____

We have seen how Stephen had allowed the Holy Spirit to control his life. He did not feel hatred or bitterness toward his enemies. Saul, on the other hand, had developed many feelings of hatred, bitterness, and pride.

A 1. Read 1 Peter 2:1 and copy this verse below to see what the Bible says we should do with the kinds of attitudes Saul demonstrated.

_____

_____

2. Make sure you know the meanings of the words in this verse. Write the meanings in the blanks provided.

- Malice: _____

  _____

- Guile: _____

  _____

- Hypocrisy: _____

  _____

- Envy: _____

  _____

- Evil speaking or slander: _____

  _____

Building Your Life Castle

The Word of God teaches us that we do not have to act and think like Saul did. The Holy Spirit who comes to live in us when we receive Jesus Christ as our Savior can change our attitudes and feelings toward others.

B 1. Can you tell of a time in which you had a wrong attitude and then let God change your attitude and feelings?

_____

_____

2. In the next few lessons, you will learn how God changed Saul's life. You will see how Saul received Christ as his Savior and how God changed all his attitudes. How has God changed your life and attitudes? _____

_____

LESSON 30
Saul's Conversion

VOCABULARY

On The Road To Damascus

A. In this lesson we are going to study Acts 9 to learn how God worked to show Saul he needed Jesus Christ as his Savior.

1. As a review from the last lesson, what was Saul's attitude toward Christians? _____
_____

2. Read Acts 9:1–2. Why was Saul going to Damascus? _____
_____

But then, as Saul came close to Damascus, a miracle took place in Saul's life. A light from heaven began to shine around the spot on which Saul stood.

B. In the chart below, write the words that were spoken to help you understand what God did.

Acts 9	Who spoke?	What was said?
1. Verse 4	Jesus	
2. Verse 5	Saul	
3. Verse 5	Jesus	
4. Verse 6	Jesus	

125

1. ✏️ According to verse 7, what did the men who were with Paul see and hear?

   _____
   _____

2. ✏️ What did God cause Saul to suffer for three days to make Himself even more real to Saul (vs. 8–9)? _____

Now that Saul had trusted Christ and had the Holy Spirit living in him, his life changed. He was now excited about the things of the Lord Jesus and wanted everyone to know what had happened to him.

3. ✏️ Read Acts 9:20. Just a few days later, what was Saul doing? _____
   _____

4. ✏️ Where was he doing this? _____

The Persecutor Is Persecuted

Saul immediately had many problems. He had become a Christian, but the Christians were afraid of him. Many of them thought he was tricking them and was still trying to kill them. They did not trust him.

The Jews were against Saul now because he no longer believed the way they did. According to Jewish tradition, if a person turned away from the Jewish faith, they were disowned. That meant that they were no longer accepted by even their own families. It was as if they had died. Some families even had funerals for those who had turned away from the Jewish traditions. Many of Saul's family and friends probably disowned him for becoming a Christian.

A ✏️ Saul, the former persecutor, now faced persecution. Read the following verses and list the ways in which Saul was persecuted by both the Jews and Christians:

Acts 9	Who persecuted Saul?	What they did or felt
Verse 21		
Verse 23		
Verse 26		

Finally, the Christians accepted the fact that Saul had indeed trusted Christ and was a Christian as they were.

Saul's Second Miracle

B ✏️ Now God had prepared yet another miracle to prove in another way to Saul that Jesus Christ was God. Answer the following questions about this miracle from Acts 9:

1. Verse 12—What vision did Saul have about Ananias? _____

2. Verse 13—What had Ananias heard about Saul? _____

3. Verse 17—What did Ananias do to Saul after he entered into his house? _____

4. Verse 18—What happened to Saul then? _____

God's Purpose For Saul's Life

We learned earlier this year that God has a purpose for every life He has made. Your life is very important to Him. He designed you to do something very, very special for Him.

When God designed Saul, He had a special purpose for his life also. Saul did not understand these things for many years. In fact, he had lived his life doing just the opposite of what God wanted him to do. But God had not changed His mind. Read Acts 9:15. Here God explains His purpose for Saul's life.

A. What was this purpose? _____

_____

Building Your Life Castle

Even though Saul had not understood for many years that he was wrong and was living in sin, it was not an excuse. He was still responsible for his actions before God. Some people will not admit when they do wrong. They say they did not know their sin was wrong, or they blame someone else for their actions. But each one of us is responsible for our own conduct before God. Excuses will not take the sin out of our lives. What is the only way that we can rid ourselves of sin as Saul did? We must trust Christ as our Savior and be forgiven of all our sins.

B. After Saul was saved, God changed his heart. Complete the puzzle below dealing with the heart and consider this question: "Is my heart right before God?"

1. Blessed are the **(4 across)** in heart (Matthew 5:8).
2. Love the Lord your God with all your **(3 down)** (Mark 12:30).
3. Even when a selfish man says, "Eat and drink," he is **(5 across)** about himself (Proverbs 23:7).
4. God has put **(6 across)** in our hearts (Psalm 4:7).
5. God knows the **(2 across)** of the heart (Psalm 44:21).
6. Solomon prayed for a **(1 down)** heart to judge God's people (1 Kings 3:9).

Word List

| Discerning | Secrets | Heart | Pure | Thinking | Gladness |

128

LESSON 31
Paul's Missionary Journeys

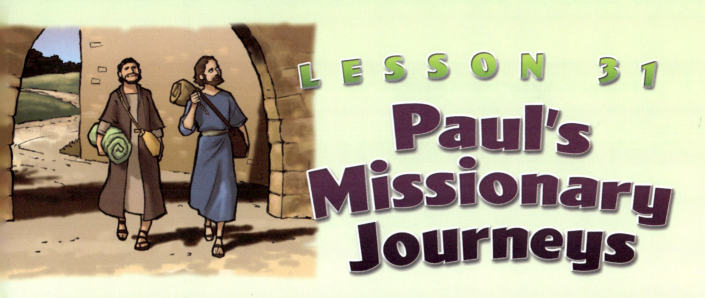

VOCABULARY

A. Saul and two other men, Barnabas and John Mark, had been preaching the gospel of Jesus Christ. Now God was ready to begin the next stage of His great purpose for Saul's life. Saul was to bring the gospel to the Gentiles.

1. ✏ Write the meaning of the word "Gentile" and tell what people Saul was to preach to.

   _____

2. ✏ Read Acts 13:2–4. Who separated Saul and Barnabas apart for this ministry? _____

3. ✏ To what was Saul's name changed at the beginning of this ministry (Acts 13:9)? _____

The First Missionary Journey

Paul made four missionary journeys during his ministry. We are going to see where God took Paul and how He used him on each of these journeys.

B. ✏ The numbers on the chart below match the numbers on the map at the end of this lesson. Write on the map the name of each place Paul visited as we read about it. We are not going to name every place Paul visited, but we will learn about the most important places.

Acts	Place	What happened here
13:1	1.	This is where Paul began his journey.
13:5	2.	
13:6, 9	3.	Saul's name was changed to _____.

129

A

Acts	Place	What happened here
1. 13:14, 50	4.	
2. 14:1	5.	
3. 14:8–10	6.	
4. 14:19	6a.	

From here they retraced their steps back to Antioch in Syria, the city from which they started. During this journey, Paul and Barnabas covered about 1,500 miles. This journey lasted two years.

The Second Missionary Journey

B Read Acts 15:36. What was the purpose for the first part of this second journey?

_____

_____

This time Paul did not go to the island of Cyprus. Instead he traveled by land from Antioch to the churches in Asia Minor. Find Asia Minor on the map. Asia Minor is part of what is now Turkey.

On this journey, Paul established many churches in cities you will recognize. Write in the names of cities 7–10 on the map. This missionary journey was much longer than his first. Paul was gone about three years and traveled over 3,000 miles. Later, Paul would write letters to the churches he established on this missionary journey. These letters are included in the New Testament and name the churches from these cities. In the chart below, write the names of the New Testament epistles Paul sent to the church in these cities.

C

Cities	New Testament Epistles
1. 7. Philippi	
2. 8. Thessalonica	
3. 9. Corinth	
4. 10. Ephesus	

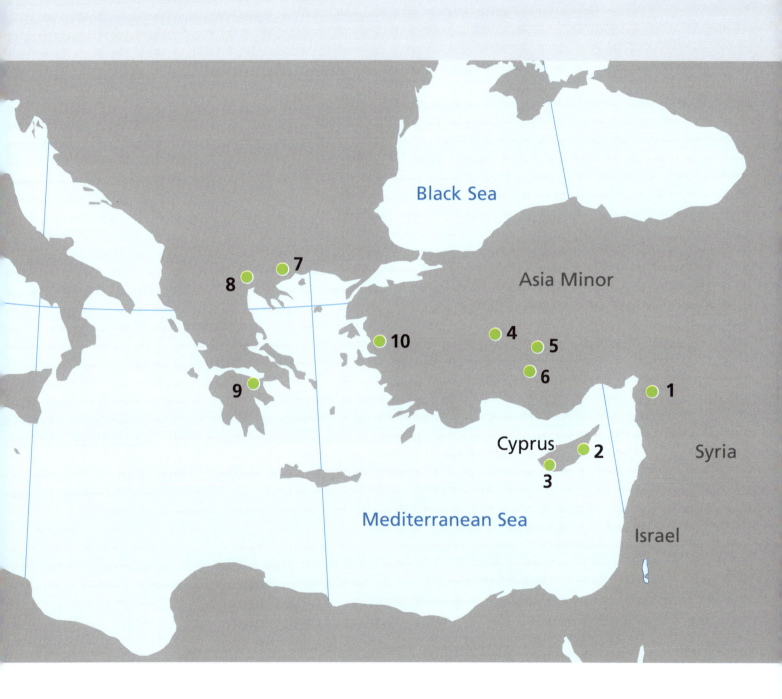

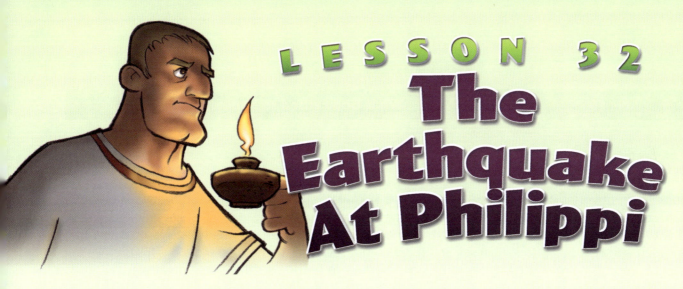

LESSON 32
The Earthquake At Philippi

During Paul's second missionary journey, an incident happened that truly shows the great character of the Apostle Paul. It shows that the Holy Spirit was at work in his life to help him in his ministry.

Paul Arrives At Philippi

These events happened at Philippi. Paul and Silas were traveling together and were preaching to some women. A woman named Lydia was saved, and she and her household were baptized. Paul and Silas went to stay at her home to rest. While there, they continued to preach the gospel message. Soon some people who made money from fortunetelling were upset by their preaching and brought them to the Roman rulers.

As you study what happened, you will see that the responses of Paul and Silas were very important to God. First you will see the problem that they faced, how they responded to the problem, and how God answered their prayers and overcame their problem.

The Problem

A

Acts 16	Problems Paul and Silas faced
1. Verse 19–21	
2. Verses 22–24	

The Response

B

Acts 16	How Paul and Silas responded
1. Verse 25	

Paul and Silas were practicing the truths found in 1 Peter 1:6–8. What were they doing that these verses talk about? _____

_____

133

God's Intervention

A.

Acts 16	What God caused to happen
1. Verses 26–28	

Look again at verses 27–28. Notice that Paul and Silas were still in the prison even though they could easily have left after the earthquake. During those times, if prisoners escaped, the jailer would be killed. It was his responsibility to make sure this did not happen. The jailer assumed that his prisoners had escaped and was going to kill himself so he would not face the shame of execution. This is why Paul told him not to harm himself. Because Paul and Silas stayed, God used them in a great way.

The Result

Acts 16	Results of Paul's ministry
2. Verses 29–34	

The One Condition Of Salvation

In verse 30, the Philippian jailer asked Paul and Silas what he needed to do to be saved. Paul gave the jailer a very simple answer. There is only one thing a person must do to become a Christian.

B. 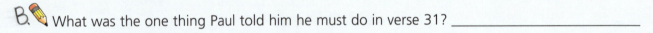 What was the one thing Paul told him he must do in verse 31? _____

_____

Building Your Life Castle

1. Have you believed on the Lord Jesus Christ as the Philippian jailer did? _____

2. Has God saved you? _____

If you have believed in Jesus Christ as your Lord and Savior, then you have the Holy Spirit living inside you just as Paul did. You can learn to walk as Paul did, allowing the Holy Spirit to control your actions and attitudes.

3. When Paul was in the jail at Philippi, how did the Holy Spirit help him to respond?

_____

_____

4. Think of a problem you have had recently. Perhaps it was a problem with a brother or sister or friend. Perhaps it was with your schoolwork or chores. Think about how you handled your problem, and think how the Holy Spirit could help you to respond to such a problem in a better way.

a. **My problem:**

b. **How I responded:**

c. **How I should respond next time:**

LESSON 33
Paul Faces Opposition

VOCABULARY

In Ephesians 5:18–21, God gives us a command to follow and some results we will experience if we obey His command.

✏️ **The Command:** (vs. 18b) _____

_____

✏️ **The Results:**

a. ● Verse 19: _____

_____

b. ● Verse 20: _____

_____

c. ● Verse 21: _____

_____

We have already studied enough about Paul's life to see that the Holy Spirit did change his life and attitudes. As we continue to see some of the things that happened to him, think about the fruit of the Spirit in his life. Many, many tribulations came to him as he went on his journeys, but the Holy Spirit continually gave him the right reactions.

People React To Paul's Preaching

Read the verses listed below. In each situation, you will learn of opposition that Paul met as he preached the gospel. In the first column, explain the problems Paul faced. In the second column, explain Paul's reaction to the problems. (Note: All references are from the Book of Acts.)

#	Paul's opposition	Paul's reactions
1	a. 13:44–45	b. 13:46
2	a. 13:50	b. 13:51–52
3	a. 14:5	b. 14:6–7
4	a. 14:19	b. 14:20
5	a. 17:5	b. 17:10
6	a. 21:30–33	b. 21:39–40
7	a. 27:40–43	b. 28:1–10

Paul—A Man With A Thankful Heart

In spite of all the trials and tribulations that the Apostle Paul faced, he always seemed to be able to find something for which he could be thankful. Read the following verses, all from the writings of Paul, and complete the puzzle below to learn more about the attitude of thanksgiving that was a consistent part of Paul's life.

Across

1. Paul was thankful for the _____ of God (1 Corinthians 1:4).
2. Paul was thankful for the way the Thessalonians had _____ the Word of God (1 Thessalonians 2:13).
3. Paul showed his thankfulness by _____ certain people in his prayers (Philemon 4).
4. Paul was thankful that he spoke in _____ (1 Corinthians 14:18).
5. Paul was thankful for what God had done through his _____ (Acts 21:19).
6. Paul was thankful that he had not _____ many so that people could not accuse him of trying to make a name for himself (1 Corinthians 1:14–15).
7. With Paul there was a connection between his thanksgiving and his _____ (Ephesians 1:16).
8. Paul was thankful for the _____ that God gives (1 Corinthians 15:57).
9. Paul was thankful that God made him able to share in the _____ of the saints (Colossians 1:12).
10. Paul _____ in the Lord for how the Philippian believers took care of his needs (Philippians 4:10).

Down

11. Paul was thankful every time he _____ the Philippians (Philippians 1:3).

Building Your Life Castle

Paul had so many "bad" things happen to him that most people would not have continued to praise God. But Paul was the writer of God's words in the Book of Ephesians that you studied at the beginning of this lesson. He had learned to let the Holy Spirit fill (control) him. The Bible says that all good gifts come from God alone (James 1:17). Let's learn to praise the Lord continually for His goodness to us instead of thinking about the problems we have.

✏️ List as many things as possible that you have to be thankful for to show God that you are learning to let the Holy Spirit teach you to be thankful.

_____
_____
_____
_____
_____
_____
_____
_____
_____

LESSON 34
Paul's Final Journeys

VOCABULARY

Paul's Third Missionary Journey

On this journey Paul returned to visit many of the churches he had started. Many interesting things happened on this journey. He preached and saw many miracles of God through his work.

Read the verses listed in the chart below, tell where the event took place, and then explain the events that occurred in each place. This will show you some of the interesting things that happened on this journey.

Acts	Place	Events
1. 18:23	a.	b.
2. 19:1, 11–12	a.	b.
3. 19:17–19	a.	b.
4. 20:6–12	a.	b.

A Idol Worship In Ephesus

During this journey, Paul spent much time preaching to those who worshiped idols. Find Acts 19 and begin reading about the idol worship of the people in verse 24.

This verse talks about a man named Demetrius who was a silversmith. This meant that he made his living by making images of the temple and the goddess that the people worshiped. The people would purchase these silver pieces to carry with them.

1. What was the name of the goddess they worshiped?

   _____

2. We can see in verse 25 why the craftsmen were upset. They had become very wealthy through making and selling these images, and now Paul was a threat to them. According to verse 26, what had Paul been saying to the people?

   _____

   _____

3. Verses 27 and 28 show how these people felt about their worship of their idol. What did they cry out? _____ !

There was great confusion and a great uproar among the people against Paul's teaching concerning idols. Finally, the crowd calmed down, and Paul left the city of Ephesus. But, again and again, through his travels, Paul found that people all over Asia believed in idols and worshiped stone images. He preached to all that Christ alone can bring salvation. Finally, God led Paul back to Jerusalem.

Paul's Fourth Missionary Journey

Paul began his fourth missionary journey as a prisoner. He was being taken to jail in Rome. But from God's point of view, this was really the beginning of a very important missionary journey. God wanted Paul in Rome for a definite purpose.

B. Now turn to Acts 28, which is the last chapter in the Book of Acts. Begin reading at verse 16 to answer the following:

1. How was Paul kept prisoner (vs. 16)? _____

   _____

A. Read verses 17–19. Write the answers to these questions using quotes from these verses.

1. Had Paul committed any crime? _____

2. Of whom was he a prisoner? _____

3. Would the Romans let Paul go? _____

4. Who caused Paul to have to appeal to Caesar? _____

B. 1. Read verse 20. What was God's purpose for having Paul taken to Rome? _____

2. Paul tried to preach to the Jews about Jesus, but they would not believe the gospel. How did Paul explain this (vs. 27)? _____

3. Since the Jews would not listen to the gospel, to whom did Paul preach (vs. 28)? _____

4. Who are the Gentiles? _____

Paul stayed in Rome for two years under arrest. He was not in a jail but was kept as a prisoner in a house. This was a great kindness provided to him by God. During this time Paul wrote letters that have become a part of our Bible. We have mentioned these places before when we studied Paul's second missionary trip. Now he writes to help these churches in their Christian lives.

During these two years, Paul was not idle. He not only wrote these letters to the churches, but God also gave him the freedom to preach the gospel to many people. His prison became a church for many people. Many of the Roman rulers heard the gospel during this time as well as others who were able to visit him.

Building Your Life Castle

Read the last few verses of the Book of Acts. The book closes so suddenly that it could appear to be unfinished. But the ideas of this book could not be finished on the pages of the Bible because the history of the church continues on. The heroes of the church and the missionary work that Paul started are still going on. New chapters are still being written to this story, even though the Bible itself is complete. It will continue to be so until God's missionary plan for the world has been completed, and Christ appears as Ruler of all.

1. Copy the last verse in the Book of Acts. This is also to be our purpose on earth because God has called us all to be missionaries for Him. _____
   _____
   _____

2. Now read Matthew 24:14. How long does Jesus Christ intend that His gospel be preached?
   _____

Christ Himself gave us this purpose for our lives. The Great Commission was not given only to people like Paul. It was given to us all. Read the Great Commission in Matthew 28:19–20 as it was given by Christ Himself.

3. What do these verses say we are to do? _____
   _____
   _____

4. What are you doing to obey the Great Commission? _____
   _____

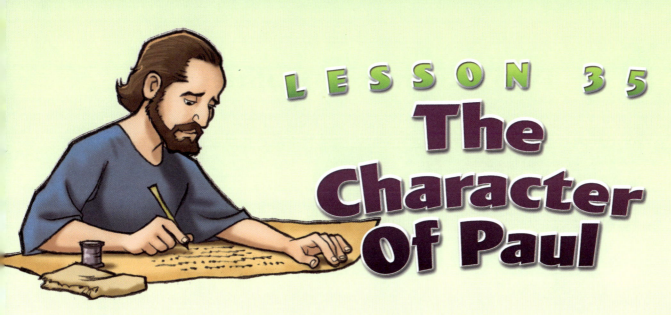

LESSON 35
The Character Of Paul

It is very important that we understand how important the Apostle Paul was for our lives. God was able to use him to fulfill many purposes. Because of Paul:

- The Gentiles received the gospel.
- Much of the New Testament was written.
- We can learn how to live the Christian life.
- We can learn how to endure tribulations.
- We see the importance of missionary work.

My Grace Is Sufficient For You

Paul is indeed very, very important to all of us. He showed us that Jesus Christ can give us everything we need.

1. How did Paul describe how important Christ was to him in 2 Corinthians 12:9? _____
_____
_____

Paul had learned to let Christ take care of him in all circumstances. Very few people have had to endure all that Paul had to endure. But in every situation, Paul knew that Christ was with him and would give him the strength he needed.

2. Read 2 Corinthians 11:24–28. As you read these verses, see how many areas of tribulation you can find that Paul endured in his journeys. Make a list of these as you read. _____
_____
_____
_____
_____
_____

Paul's Character Qualities

It was the character of God inside of Paul that enabled him to be used for such a great purpose. As you complete the following puzzle, think how each character quality was an important part of Paul's life:

Word Box

Obedience | Perseverance | Endurance (not giving up) | Courage | Joy | Industry (working hard) | Faithful | Love

Across

1. Paul was willing to work hard (Acts 20:34).
2. Paul willingly did what God asked him to do (Acts 26:19).
5. Paul finished his course and kept the faith (2 Timothy 4:7).
7. Paul was willing to suffer anything in order to further the gospel (Acts 22:24–25).
8. Paul waited for God's timing in all things (2 Corinthians 12:12).

Down

3. Paul would not give up, no matter what the circumstances (2 Timothy 2:10).
4. Paul did all his work with a joyful attitude (Philippians 4:4).
6. Paul gave his life for others (1 Corinthians 16:24).

Music Curriculum

September Hymn

How Great Thou Art

O Lord my God! When I in awesome wonder
Consider all the works Thy hands have made,
I see the stars, I hear the mighty thunder,
Thy pow'r thro'out the universe displayed,

When thro' the woods and forest glades I wander
And hear the birds sing sweetly in the trees;
When I look down from lofty mountain grandeur,
And hear the brook, and feel the gentle breeze;

And when I think that God, His Son not sparing,
Sent Him to die—I scarce can take it in;—
That on the cross, my burden gladly bearing,
He bled and died, to take away my sin;

When Christ shall come with shout of acclamation
And take me home—what joy shall fill my heart!
Then I shall bow in humble adoration,
And there proclaim, my God, how great Thou art!

Chorus

Then sings my soul, my Savior God to Thee;
How great Thou art, how great Thou art!
Then sings my soul, my Savior God to Thee;
How great Thou art, how great Thou art!

September Choruses

I Belong To Jesus

I belong to Jesus, He set me free
And He keeps me singing sweet melody,
Fills my life with sunshine, whate'er betide;
I belong to Jesus, He's by my side.

Hallelu, Hallelujah!

Hallelu, hallelu, hallelu, hallelujah! Praise ye the Lord!
Hallelu, hallelu, hallelu, hallelujah! Praise ye the Lord!
Praise ye the Lord, hallelujah! Praise ye the Lord, hallelujah!
Praise ye the Lord, hallelujah! Praise ye the Lord!

October Hymn

The Old Rugged Cross

On a hill far away stood an old rugged cross,
The emblem of suffering and shame;
And I love that old cross where the dearest and best
For a world of lost sinners was slain.

Oh, that old rugged cross, so despised by the world,
Has a wondrous attraction for me;
For the dear Lamb of God left His glory above
To bear it to dark Calvary.

In the old rugged cross, stained with blood so divine,
A wondrous beauty I see;
For 'twas on that old cross Jesus suffered and died
To pardon and sanctify me.

To the old rugged cross I will ever be true,
Its shame and reproach gladly bear;
Then He'll call me some day to my home far away,
Where His glory forever I'll share

Chorus
So I'll cherish the old rugged cross,
Till my trophies at last I lay down;
I will cling to the old rugged cross,
And exchange it some day for a crown.

October Choruses

There Were Twelve Disciples

There were twelve disciples Jesus called to help Him:
Simon Peter, Andrew, James, his brother John;
Philip, Thomas, Matthew, James, the son Alphaeus,
Thaddeus, Simon, Judas and Bartholomew.
He has called us too, He has called us too;
We are His disciples; I am one, are you?
He has called us too, He has called us too;
We are His disciples; we His work must do.

The Good Shepherd

We children have learned a sweet story,
From the Book far more precious than gold;
'Tis of Jesus the Shepherd, who loves us,
And His beautiful heavenly fold.

That kind loving shepherd is watching
And caring for us here below;
And He says "we should love one another"
And like Him "deeds of kindness to show."

Chorus

Yes, Jesus, the Good Shepherd loves us,
And tenderly cares each day;
Yes, Jesus the Good Shepherd loves us,
And leads us each step of the way.

November Hymn

America The Beautiful

O beautiful for spacious skies, for amber waves of grain,
For purple mountain majesties above the fruited plain!
America! America! God shed His grace on thee,
And crown thy good with brotherhood from sea to shining sea.

O beautiful for pilgrim feet, whose stern, impassioned stress
A thoroughfare for freedom beat across the wilderness!
America! America! God mend thine ev'ry flaw,
Confirm thy soul in self-control, thy liberty in law.

O beautiful for heroes proved in liberating strife,
Who more than self their country loved and mercy more than life!
America! America! May God thy gold refine,
Till all success be nobleness, and ev'ry gain divine.

O beautiful for patriot dream that sees, beyond the years,
Thine alabaster cities gleam—undimmed by human tears!
America! America! God shed His grace on thee,
And crown thy good with brotherhood from sea to shining sea.

November Choruses

Jesus, Jesus, Is Our Song

Jesus, Jesus, is our song today;
Jesus, Jesus, all along the way;
He will guide us ever,
He will fail us never,
Till we reach our happy home above.
Jesus, Jesus, blessed Friend divine;
Jesus, Jesus, how His light doth shine;
We will shout and sing His wondrous love,
While marching 'neath His banner glorious.

Fishers Of Men

I will make you fishers of men, fishers of men, fishers of men;
I will make you fishers of men if you follow Me;
If you follow Me, if you follow Me,
I will make you fishers of men if follow Me.

Hear Christ calling, "Come unto Me,
Come unto Me, Come unto Me;"
Hear Christ calling, "Come unto Me, I will give you rest,
I will give you rest, I will give you rest;"
Hear Christ calling, "Come unto Me, I will give you rest."

We Thank Our Loving Father, God

We thank our loving Father, God, who gives us ev'rything;
Who sends the sunshine and the show'rs, and makes rich harvests spring.
He clothes the lilies of the field, He feeds each bird and beast;
And all may share His tender care, the greatest and the least.

December Hymn

O Little Town Of Bethlehem

O little town of Bethlehem,
How still we see thee lie!
Above thy deep and dreamless sleep
The silent stars go by.
Yet in thy dark streets shineth
The everlasting Light;
The hopes and fears of all the years
Are met in thee tonight.

For Christ is born of Mary,
And gathered all above,
While mortals sleep, the angels keep
Their watch of wond'ring love,
O morning stars, together
Proclaim the holy birth!
And praises sing to God the King,
And peace to men on earth.

How silently, how silently,
The wondrous gift is giv'n!
So God imparts to human hearts
The blessing of His heav'n.
No ear may hear His coming,
But in this world of sin,
Where meek souls will receive Him still
The dear Christ enters in.

O holy Child of Bethlehem!
Descend to us, we pray;
Cast out our sin, and enter in;
Be born in us today.
We hear the Christmas angels
The great glad tidings tell;
O come to us, abide with us,
Our Lord Emmanuel.

January Hymn

Amazing Grace

Amazing grace! how sweet the sound
That saved a wretch like me!
I once was lost, but now am found,
Was blind, but now I see.

'Twas grace that taught my heart to fear,
And grace my fears relieved;
How precious did that grace appear
The hour I first believed!

Through many dangers, toils, and snares,
I have already come;
'Tis grace hath brought me safe thus far,
And grace will lead me home

The Lord has promised good to me,
His word my hope secures;
He will my shield and portion be
As long as life endures.

Yea, when this flesh and heart shall fail,
And mortal life shall cease,
I shall possess, within the veil,
A life of joy and peace.

January Choruses

I Am The Door

I am the Door, by Me if any man enter in;
I am the Door, by Me if any man enter in,
He shall be saved, he shall be saved,
And shall go in and out finding pasture, green pasture, green pasture,
He shall go in and out finding pasture.

His Sheep Am I

In God's green pastures feeding, by His cool waters lie,
Soft in the evening walk my Lord and I.
All the sheep of His pasture fare so wondrously fine.
His sheep am I.

Waters cool, *(in the valley,) pastures green *(on the mountain,)
In the evening walk my Lord and I;
Dark the night, *(in the valley,) rough the way, *(on the mountain,)
Step by step my Lord and I.

*Divide the class and have one group sing this part.

January Chorus

God's Clock

I set my life by God's great clock, His time is always right;
He times the wind, the rain, the snow, He times the day and night.

God times the winter and the spring, the summer and the fall;
The sun and moon and stars are His—His hand rules over all!

God times the blossom on the bough, the flight of bird and bee;
How safely I may trust His love to choose what's best for me!

I set my life by God's great clock, He's never fast or slow;
He plans a perfect day for those who seek His will to know.

Chorus

God's time *(tick tock) is right, *(tick tock) there's none so wise as He,
His hand upholds the whole wide world; He knows what's best for me. *(tick tock)
(After 4 times repeating the chorus) I want His best for me.

*Divide the class and have one group sing this part.

February Hymn

I Love To Tell The Story

I love to tell the story of unseen things above,
Of Jesus and His glory, of Jesus and His love.
I love to tell the story, because I know 'tis true;
It satisfies my longings as nothing else can do.

I love to tell the story, more wonderful it seems
Than all the golden fancies of all our golden dreams.
I love to tell the story, it did so much for me;
And that is just the reason I tell it now to thee.

I love to tell the story, 'tis pleasant to repeat
What seems, each time I tell it, more wonderfully sweet.
I love to tell the story, for some have never heard
The message of salvation from God's own Holy Word.

I love to tell the story, for those who know it best
Seem hungering and thirsting to hear it like the rest.
And when, in scenes of glory, I sing the new, new song,
'Twill be the old, old story that I have loved so long.

Chorus

I love to tell the story, 'twill be my theme in glory
To tell the old, old story of Jesus and His love.

February Choruses

For God So Loved The World
For God so loved the world,
He gave His only Son,
To die on Calv'ry's tree,
From sin to set me free;
Some day He's coming back,
What glory that will be!
Wonderful His love to me.

I Am The Resurrection
I am the resurrection and the life,
He that believeth in Me tho' he were dead,
Yet shall he live, yet shall he live,
And whosoever liveth and believeth in Me shall never, never die,
Shall never, never die.

Wait On The Lord
Wait on the Lord, be of good courage.
Wait on the Lord, be of good courage.
Wait on the Lord, be of good courage,
And He will strengthen your heart.
And He will strengthen your heart.
And He will strengthen your heart.
Wait on the Lord, be of good courage.
Wait, I say, on the Lord.
Wait, I say, on the Lord.
Wait, I say, on the Lord.

March Hymn

What A Friend We Have In Jesus

What a Friend we have in Jesus, all our sins and griefs to bear!
What a privilege to carry ev'rything to God in prayer!
O what peace we often forfeit, O what needless pain we bear,
All because we do not carry ev'rything to God in prayer!

Have we trials and temptations? Is there trouble anywhere?
We should never be discouraged—take it to the Lord in prayer.
Can we find a Friend so faithful who will all our sorrows share?
Jesus knows our ev'ry weakness—take it to the Lord in prayer.

Are we weak and heavy laden, cumbered with a load of care?
Precious Savior, still our refuge—take it to the Lord in prayer.
Do thy friends despise, forsake thee? Take it to the Lord in prayer;
In His arms He'll take and shield thee—thou wilt find a solace there.

March Choruses

Rolled Away

Rolled away, rolled away, rolled away,
Ev'ry burden of my heart rolled away;
Rolled away, rolled away, rolled away,
Ev'ry burden of my heart rolled away.
All my sin had to go
'Neath the crimson flow.
Rolled away, rolled away, rolled away;
Ev'ry burden of my heart rolled away!

He Holds My Hand

He holds my hand, Jesus holds my hand;
Safely to heaven He leads the way,
He is my keeper from day to day;
He holds my hand, Jesus holds my hand;
The road may be long,
But my Savior is strong,
And He holds my hand.

We Will Run The Race Of Life

We will run, run, run the race of life;
We will run, run, run for Jesus;
We will love and serve Him ev'ry day,
As we run, run, run for Him.

April Hymn

My Faith Looks Up To Thee

My faith looks up to Thee, Thou Lamb of Calvary, Savior divine!
Now hear me while I pray, take all my guilt away,
O let me from this day be wholly Thine!

May Thy rich grace impart strength to my fainting heart, my zeal inspire;
As Thou hast died for me, O may my love to Thee
Pure, warm and changeless be, a living fire!

While life's dark maze I tread, and griefs around me spread, be Thou my Guide;
Bid darkness turn to day, wipe sorrow's tears away,
Nor let me ever stray from Thee aside.

When ends life's transient dream, when death's cold, sullen stream shall o'er me roll;
Blest Savior, then, in love, fear and distrust remove;
O bear me safe above, a ransomed soul!

April Choruses

One Door And Only One

One door, and only one,
And yet its sides are two;
"Inside" and "outside."
On which side are you?
One door, and only one,
And yet its sides are two;
I'm on the inside,
On which side are you?

Prayer Is The Key

How sweet to hide ourselves away
Where only God is near,
And breathe our inmost secret tho'ts
Where only He can hear.

There's not a wound that sorrow gives,
There's not a pain we feel,
But if we go to God in prayer,
His love will gently heal.

How oft in prayer a sudden light
Breaks forth thro' clouded skies,
And on its beams, to Him we love,
Our longing souls arise.

In prayer we find calm relief
From every throb of pain;
And they who trust in Christ, our Lord,
Shall never trust in vain.

Chorus

Prayer is the key, the only key,
To heav'n's unfailing store;
Faith is the hand that guides our own,
But prayer unlocks the door.

Down In My Heart

I have the joy, joy, joy, joy, down in my heart,
Down in my heart, down in my heart,
I have the joy, joy, joy, joy, down in my heart,
Down in my heart to stay.

I have the peace that passeth understanding, down in my heart,
Down in my heart, down in my heart,
I have the peace that passeth understanding, down in my heart,
Down in my heart to stay.

I have the love of Jesus, love of Jesus, down in my heart,
Down in my heart, down in my heart,
I have the love of Jesus, love of Jesus, down in my heart,
Down in my heart to stay.

For there is therefore now no condemnation, down in my heart,
Down in my heart, down in my heart,
For there is therefore now no condemnation, down in my heart,
Down in my heart to stay.

May Hymn

Stand Up, Stand Up For Jesus

Stand up, stand up for Jesus, ye soldiers of the cross!
Lift high His royal banner—it must not suffer loss.
From vict'ry unto vict'ry His army shall He lead,
Till ev'ry foe is vanquished and Christ is Lord indeed.

Stand up, stand up for Jesus, the trumpet call obey;
Forth to the mighty conflict in this His glorious day.
Ye that are men now serve Him against unnumbered foes;
Let courage rise with danger, and strength to strength oppose.

Stand up, stand up for Jesus, stand in His strength alone;
Put on the gospel armor, each piece put on with prayer;
Where duty calls, or danger, be never wanting there.
The arm of flesh will fail you—ye dare not trust your own.

Stand up, stand up for Jesus, the strife will not be long;
This day the noise of battle—the next, the victor's song.
To him that overcometh a crown of life shall be:
He with the King of glory shall reign eternally.

May Choruses

One God And One Mediator

For there is one God and one mediator between God and men,
For there is one God and one mediator, the Man, Christ Jesus.
Who gave Himself a ransom for us all;
Who gave Himself a ransom for us all;
Who gave Himself a ransom for us all;
Oh, what a wonderful Savior!
For there is one God and one mediator between God and men,
For there is one God and one mediator, the Man, Christ Jesus.

Following Jesus

Following Jesus, ever day by day,
Nothing can harm me when He leads the way;
Sunshine or shadow, whate'er befall,
Jesus my Savior is my All in All.

The Wise May Bring Their Learning

The wise may bring their learning, the rich may bring their wealth,
And some may bring their greatness, and some bring strength and health;
We, too, would bring our treasures to offer to the King;
We have no wealth or learning; what shall we children bring?

We'll bring Him hearts that love Him; we'll bring Him thankful praise,
And young souls meekly striving to walk in holy ways;
And these shall be the treasures we offer to the King,
And these are gifts that even the poorest child may bring.

We'll bring the little duties we have to do each day;
We'll try our best to please Him, at home, at school, at play;
And better are these treasures to offer to our King
Than richest gifts without them; yet, these a child may bring.

Building Life Castles Scripture Memorization Sheet

Name:		Grade:	Teacher:

Week	Scripture	Due Date	Parent's Signature
1	1 Cor. 13:1		
2	1 Cor. 13:2–3		
3	1 Cor. 13:4–5		
4	1 Cor. 13:6–7		
5	**1 Cor. 13:1–7**		
6	Eph. 6:1–3		
7	Eph. 6:4–5		
8	**Eph. 6:1–5**		
9	Eph. 6:6–7		
10	Eph. 6:8–9		
11	**Eph. 6:6–9**		
12	Psalm 1:1–2		
13	Psalm 1:3–4		
14	Psalm 1:5–6		
15	**Psalm 1:1–6**		
16	Phil. 4:4–5		
17	Phil. 4:6–7		
18	Phil. 4:8–9		
19	**Phil. 4:4–9**		
20	John 1:1–2		
21	John 1:3–4		
22	John 1:5–6		
23	John 1:7–8		
24	**John 1:1–8**		
25	John 1:9–10		
26	John 1:11–12		
27	John 1:13–14		
28	**John 1:9–14**		
29	John 1:15–16		
30	John 1:17–18		
31	**John 1:15–18**		
32	Psalm 23:1–2		
33	Psalm 23:3–4		
34	Psalm 23:5–6		
35	**Psalm 23:1–6**		